Look What They've Done To My Church

Look What They've Done To My Church

Leonard Urban

A Campion Book

Loyola University Press
Chicago 60657

Loyola University Press
3441 North Ashland Avenue
Chicago, Illinois 60657

Design by J.L. Boden

Library of Congress Cataloging in Publication Data

Urban, Leonard
    Look what they've done to my church.

    1. Catholic Church—Doctrines. 2. Catholic
Church—History—1965-   . I. Title.
BX1751.2.U73 1985   282'.09'04   85-10345
ISBN 0-8294-0499-6

To Peter, Kathy, and Elizabeth—to
all who have offered encouragement
and the hand of support.

Contents

Preface

Some years ago a woman came to the rectory to visit. She "happened by" because she was in the area and had been thinking of talking to someone for a long time. She had been a Catholic all her life. But due to circumstances, divorce and its panoply of troubles, the need of a job, and the task of single parent child rearing, she somehow got away from the church. It wasn't a conscious rejection. It was just that too many other priorities came into her life. Perhaps there was not enough time.

While she was "gone," a whole rash of changes took place. When she did go to church, Christmas and such days, she seemed at a distance from what she had known. She found that others felt the same way, in a quandary, mystified by what was happening. Was there an explanation?

Her departure, if that's a good word, took place seventeen years before our conversation. She had a long list of questions to ask which began with her status in the church and wove around liturgy, sacraments, belief, and new approaches to the gospel. We talked for a couple hours, exchanging notions and conferring. I got a few books off the shelf and read a line or two to her.

At the end of our conversation, she asked if there were a book she could read which touched the subjects we had discussed. I said there were many books available, but none which would treat our discussion under one cover. In a flush of what now seems to have been unforgivable arrogance, I suggested that I might write one, a book for the times and seasons of people in her position. As I thought of it, it seemed to me that the people in the pew, the faithful adherents to the faith, had been short shrifted and deserved something more than the technical treatises on theology which were available.

There are any number of people who have absented themselves from the church. There are others who would be pleased with a better explanation of what has happened to their church over the past twenty-five years. Still others would welcome some thoughts about developments in religion and God's presence in the modern world. Questions will never end; they take new turns and demand answers which offer some assurance.

This book is an effort to respond to the questions of those who have no special theological background, the vast majority of the people. It seeks to address issues and subjects which are pertinent and familiar to almost everyone. It does not demand agreement; it offers no arguments which are irrefutable; and in no way does it presume to be the last word in religion. Hopefully, it is a simple treatment of what has too often turned out to be a complex topic. After reading this, you will probably agree that the original message which God offered to us through Jesus was not meant to overwhelm us. There should be a genuine joy in knowing God and being a part of a faith community.

No book is written by one person. It is a compendium of experiences and people which reach back to the beginning of life itself. I am deeply grateful to those persons who by their confidence and support contributed to this work, especially those who gave assurance, accepted my absence from pastoral duties, and offered the magic of encouragement.

No pastor is right all the time. We are a people who are inclined to doctrines and certitude. Perhaps this book will offer something by way of apology to those who have been misdirected, disillusioned by religious righteousness, or made to think they had no place. This book is directed particularly to them; to the multitude of people who search, who ask for understanding and accceptance. It is my hope they will find that and more in these pages.

Leonard Urban
Frederick, Colorado

Chapter 1

Where have we been and where are we going?

If Irving's classic character, Rip Van Winkle, were a Christian, or better, a Catholic, and had taken his celebrated twenty years' nap beginning about 1958, his awakening might have been even ruder than it was in its original setting. It's an interesting hypothesis which demonstrates a few points about transitions and what change does to our lives. It all has something to say about boat rocking, about security, and about keeping up or being left out.

To continue with the analogy, it was a different church in a different world some twenty-five years ago. There it stood, on the horizons of our lives, a bulwark of strength, the invulnerable rock of Peter. Apparently in superb health, the church had weathered a thousand storms down a long corridor of battering centuries. It gave testimony to God's protective presence and withstood whatever onslaught might have dared to attack it. What could happen which hadn't happened already? The church had survived it all.

Whatever it was, heresy, faulty doctrine, or the faults of individuals in those early centuries, the church surmounted them by sheer force of righteous strength, authority, and commanding disposition. Were there dissenters who periodically rose up to call the church into question or make rash inquiries into its teachings and doctrines? The church kept its dignity and composure. At times it paused to redefine, specify, and legislate, as in the Council of Trent, the Inquisition, the voice of God voiced through the pope, the bishops, the teaching office of the church. Was it sometimes an erring pope or bishop, or the clergy wandering from well-defined paths, whose conduct could have been embarrassing, a blemish on the smooth surface of virtue and holy dignity? It all the more proved the strength of the church and its divine origins. It was a church against which the gates of hell could not prevail, which could neatly survive those tremors without its surface cracking and splitting.

With only a few minor disturbances which might require rolling over a time or two, settling in, Rip Van Winkle would have been able to sleep fairly comfortably. He would have enjoyed a relatively deep rest without too much worry. His last thoughts might have been about his church of changeless strength, that protective wing of concern over a torn and fractured world, surviving through God's visible embrace.

In yesterday's church, the laity were an obedient people who asked few questions. The church expected submission and reverence. The clergy in former days were dependable, obedient, and predictable. As in the case of the laity, they were identified by their submission to a well-defined hierarchy, beginning with the pope and descending through bishops, vicars, pastors, superiors, and assistants. Such submissive willingness to take one's place in the order was not without its merits and favors. The same or similar descriptions could be applied to the state of women. They too fit rather smoothly into a scheme thoughtfully developed and carefully sustained.

The local bishop with local authority personified the hierarchical network. He represented the approved direction of the church. The "ideal" bishop was that one who clearly modeled what came from above. The trusted anticipation was that he should be neither to the left nor right, but rather a dependable mirror of whatever was said and taught through the chain of command.

The last word in this structure was, of course, the pope, the supreme pontiff, leader of the Catholic world. It was to him that all obedience was finally due. It was by his decree and command that the entire church was directed. Together with those chosen assistants who comprised the papal household, doctrines were declared, directives issued, policies underscored, and programs initiated.

That such a framework was enormously powerful, wielding formidable persuasion, was clearly evident. Every movement, every effort was filtered through the structure, measured against inflexible standards, most times approved or rejected without recourse. A generous reliance upon imprimaturs, nihil obstats, censures, sanctions, suspensions, and even excommunications was accepted as normal. There was little questioning of the use of power, the demands of superiors, and the force of decree.

When our Catholic Rip Van Winkle's sleep began, there were distinguishing characteristics which made the church unique. The mass, ceremonies of every kind, rituals, devotions, and pious practices were all inseparable parts of the organization. It was easy to remember long confession lines and the refreshing feeling of sins forgiven. Rip might further remember the silent blinking of vigil lights in a darkening church, our presence before God even in our absence. His memory was sensitive to the scent of incense, the arresting swish of sacred vestments, silk brocade, elaborate design, the brilliant monstrance raised high over the congregation at benediction. It was a quiet church then, a few tolerated whisperings, no talking aloud, no singing please, perhaps some organ renditions, a few restricted strains from the violin at Christmas midnight liturgy, and a trained choir for special occasions.

It was all the same everywhere, an unparalleled unity found only in the Catholic church. If you walked into church in East Afghanistan, Scranton, Denver, or Bermuda, there it was, clearly, the familiar sounds of *Introibo ad altare Dei,* the visible presence of the eternal priesthood, his back to us, "Holy Mother Church" in fullness across the world, like home, like old hometown, the universal connection. We were ready, prepared, oil in our lamps, missal in hand, bound in Moroccan leather, two-columned, gold-leafed, with many ribbons.

There were seven sacraments, four cardinal virtues, six commandments of the church, twelve fruits of the Holy Spirit, seven deadly sins, and a number of other numbers. What we didn't understand about all of them, we believed on the basis of merit in believing without understanding. We received the sacraments regularly and made sure of them for others. "Get the baby baptized." "Were they married in the Church?" "Have your children received confirmation?" "One can receive the last rites up to half an hour after lingering death, up to two hours if it was sudden." "If you swallow a little water while rinsing your teeth, it breaks the fast and you may not receive communion." "Never neglect any of them. They have a grace-giving effect, even in spite of the questionable disposition of the receiver. They work automatically, they seal the soul."

It was all there, certainty in uncertain times, security in turmoil, true because the priest said it, who said the bishop said it, who said the pope said it was eternal truth, tradition, defined doctrine, tried by time and never found wanting. In defense of such truth, some suffered persecution, braved the lion, the soldier's bayonet, the coliseum, the martyr's arena.

For every question, however slippery, there was a

reasonable answer. If some suffer, they need only wait for heaven. Time passes; a drop compared to eternity. Justice comes at another time. If some have more while others have less, we simply have to leave it to God who is infinitely wise and whose ways are not ours. The church can be rich and triumphal, because it must reflect the dignity and triumph of Christ. Never mind that the Son of Man had no place to lay his head. He is risen, gloriously, and reigns triumphant in heaven.

Little wonder that Rip Van Winkle could sleep so soundly, rest so comfortably. It was a time for sleeping. It was a time for taking rest.

And while that sleeping passed from one year into the next, there began a stirring within the bosom of time and persons which would soon take away repose, awaken those in deepest slumber, and change what had remained so long unchanged, never to be the same again. Depending on one's point of view, these were the best of times and the worst of times. But few people have been unmoved or indifferent to the changes which demand recognition, response, and integration in our changing lives.

All of us, to some degree, can identify with that long sleep, see ourselves there, more or less tranquilized, in a state of partial unawareness. For some of us, the waking was gradual, keeping pace. For others, it was rude, shocking us into places where we had to ask how we had arrived and what had happened. For most, it was not easy. Welcome? Yes, in some cases; but never without the demands of growth.

What has happened in the past twenty-five years has brought into question much of what preceded in the past two thousand. What is happening now has initiated results so various and unanticipated as to be yet incalculable. We can only determine that we are at the brink of something so different as to have no parallel, so new as to be greatly surprising, a Poseidon adventure whose port and harbor we have not yet sighted.

What has happened has awakened us from sleep,

demanded some reaction, and denied our state of being neither hot nor cold. For many it has meant, not so simply, letting go, leaving the church, going away, perhaps to return in better times. For some it has meant a death-grip struggle to restore what was, vehemently resisting change, contending that God is on the side of complacency. They have admitted the new church into their lives, the same as the old, but never to the measure that it would disturb their rock-like faith.

Yet another group has left the church in order to stay. Paradoxically, they see their own lifestyles as closer to what they judge the intrinsic meaning of the gospel message to be. In the past twenty-five years thousands of priests and religious men and women have relinquished formal positions in active ministry. In their own judgment, many of them are still involved, caring, ministering, perhaps more effectively than before.

Finally, there are those who, after this time of upheaval, have chosen to stay, to continue to offer support and membership. Their decision does not rest on passivity, nor is it a desperate clinging to what was in the hope that it will soon or someday be again. Theirs is rather the acceptance of the challenge which the message of the gospel offers. Many are now seeing the church as a setting in which to exercise a personal ministry, a call to begin to live out the counsel of Jesus. This involves a decision of greater honesty, first of oneself and then of others. It is born of a studied conviction that theology can be relevant, that God can be found in people, and that there is no real distinction between religion and daily life.

The people who have made such choices see our time as one of rich opportunity. They are demanding more from those who give, and they are giving more themselves. They are seeing more objectively the weaknesses and shortcomings of the church and are yet more tolerant and patient as a group. They are not uncomfortable as a minority. They are given to witnessing and to searching for meaning in what they are doing.

These renewed people can be found in every parish,

working in inner-city projects, peace movements, Catholic Worker houses, and in small groups of nuns living in the community. Some are in team ministry, finding mutual strength in unified effort, a tolerant regard and acceptance for one another without competition and favoritism. Many are in family settings. You'll find many of them among the people in the pews, the congregated Christians who are seeking, deeply conscious that they have a gift, willing to give it in the hope that it will be accepted and cherished. They're on parish councils, social concern committees, asking for better religious education, more challenging homilies; they are a probing, value-oriented people. They see a new time, a new church whose demanding challenge is to find a better approach to so many things which need new energy. They keep asking questions, wanting more. They are looking for better explanations, for clarity in a life that has become confused and ambiguous with overwork and cultural pressures, and they are looking for the meaning of religion in the midst of it all.

If Rip Van Winkle were a Catholic and had taken his nap twenty-five years ago, these are just some of the realities he would have awakened to. There are so many more, inestimable in number and kind, sweeping in breadth and implication. If upon rising he had walked into a sampling of churches in parishes across the country, he would have found the celebrant facing the people at mass, speaking in English, the congregation actively participating, praying, talking, singing, perhaps to the strum of guitars, or the faint strains of the flute. He would have met words and realities unknown twenty-five years before: lectors, commentators, deacons, lay communion distributors, prayers of the faithful, communion in both species and in the hand, ordinary bread, banners hanging in the sanctuary, simpler vestments and altar furnishings, to mention only a few. Not the same in every parish, but enough similarity to warrant confusion and wonder.

He would be further confused by the conspicuous absence of devotions, novenas, and missions, old standbys of a time past; the further disappearance of benediction, of black vestments, and requiem masses, birettas, capes, amices, maniples, and vesting prayers, fish on Friday, the traditional days of fast and abstinence, and the pastor's black car.

He'd hear homilies different from those old days. More emphasis now on social justice, boycotts, third world problems, racial prejudice, conscience formation, personalized ministry, and new looks at old morality. He might even hear members of the congregation in dialogue with the priest, or a lay person speaking from the pulpit.

If, after so long a nap, our friend strolled into a rectory or parish center to ask about religious education, baptism, or confirmation for his child, a date for marriage, or first communion classes, his shock would undoubtedly continue. Contrary to former times when sacraments were administered without question, sometimes hastily against the possibility that the opportunity might never arise again, he might be asked to defer, learn to understand the sacrament, and prepare for receiving it first. He might even be counseled to consider the emptiness of sacraments and religious formality where there is no real conviction or faith giving evidence to the value of such practice. He might be asked not to receive a sacrament, not to be married "in the Church," for example, if it's only to please one's parents or because Grandma would have a heart attack if he didn't.

The same might be said for religious education. Our visitor would at least be exposed to some new ideas about parental involvement if religious education for the child is to be effective. In some parishes, he and his wife would be strongly encouraged to attend classes at the same time their children do. They might be given "homework," a task to be accomplished together as a family, bringing religious flavor and value into the home.

If we, like our friend Van Winkle, walked into a situation with so much unfamiliar terrain, we'd obviously have to make some choices. We might see a church banner somewhere emphatically declaring: "Not to decide is to decide." Not deciding is what some of us do when we insist on immobility or, at best, a backward plunge in the hope of security, the "good old days." And even that is a choice. So the necessity of deciding is obvious. The range of possibilities is broad, offering the opportunity of some personal satisfactions. The single requirement for any favorable choice, however, must be that we understand what we are choosing and why. The same understanding may prevail in rejecting whatever it is we reject. To make choices in any other manner is illogical and meaningless. Understanding is the key word. It is not an automatic process in us, not like the digestive or nervous system. It comes as the fruit of personal and often intense endeavor, sheer hard work. It begins with the conscious gathering of information, sorting, integrating, reviewing, and omitting hasty conclusions. It must be subject to growth and a willingness to give up what is obviously untrue. Gathering information cannot be approached without humility and freedom from prejudice.

If we had been asleep for the past twenty-five years, we would have a monumental amount of catching up to do. As a matter of fact, many of us have been at least napping while different directions were being taken. It is a new time now, a time of decision to bring into the day what has too long been left in the darkness.

What has happened in the church in the past twenty-five years clearly happened for good reasons. To understand something of those causes, to take the time to inform ourselves, is to be no more than reasonable. To make choices, to judge the value of such a gigantic transition, without honest endeavor, hastily, is to miss a basic principle: we are only human when we act rationally. It is rational, human, to respond to the internal desire for understanding; in our case, to understand what has happened in the church. It might just be that in the end what is happening is surprisingly clear and simple. And to clarify and hopefully to explain is the purpose of this book.

Chapter 2

The notion of God

There has never been a time in our recollection of history which has not been characterized by an intense questioning of the meaning of life and our purpose here. And the question has always been associated with some idea of God, whether crude and fundamental or highly refined and sophisticated: the supreme being, the creator, or the gods.

From the very beginning of our conscious awareness as human beings, we have pondered the issue in every cultural setting. The question was often approached with shattering fear, a sense of deep insecurity, and hopeless dependency on fate or chance. Life, the meaning of existence, our time here, have always been regarded with foreboding and mystery, and an abiding uncertainty of what is yet to come. We have experienced feelings of hope, desperate longing, joy in ourselves and others, helpless dependency, agonizing inability, the flush of welcome love, the rage of hatred, resistance to suffering and death, to mention only a few of the thousands of changing, mixing, and apparently endless reactions which are the unavoidable ingredients of life.

To the primitive people at the beginning of time, capricious storms that thundered down, bringing helpless terror, the inexplicable beauty of simple sunsets, the seeming futility of life in the face of sickness and death, the very stress of meeting the daily demands of hunger, cold, and nakedness were all a mixture of events that simply boggled the mind and left a wake of confusion. There had to be some explanation, some semblance of order amid the chaos. It was surely out of these dim sentiments that we began our long journey upward and away from a mere instinctive acceptance of the hodge-podge circumstances of life.

The mystery of life, its very resistance to any easy solutions, has repeatedly pushed us out of what we immediately experience to hope for the possibility that there should be something more. People have always looked upon such hopes and dark leaps as worthwhile, giving purpose to life which would otherwise be meaningless and without consequence. Is there something which moves beyond our life, a source of life itself? Is there some inner force so present that we could never exist apart from it, would simply cease to be without it?

These are questions which have preoccupied our human minds and thinking from the very beginning. They are never finished, never completely answered. Out of these questions we have formed a history of our effort to know the meaning of existence and who God is. This effort is as ancient as people themselves.

Who is God? Is God real or only the result of unsatisfied longing? Is God dead? Do we need God in our self-sufficient times?

The Christian notion of God begins in the Old Testament, with the beginnings of a small nation of unimportant people destined for greater things. From the Jewish nation was born the idea of a covenant or agreement between God and his chosen people. They consented to accept and obey God's commands; and he promised a response of care and support, just like a good parent looking after the needs of his children. It was perfectly reasonable that such demands could be justly made, since God was understood as the absolute creator of all things, the maker of everything which could be known. God had complete and final control of the universe, moving everything in a direction which accomplished a previous design. If at times God's law seemed heavy-handed, wrath-filled, and brooking no quarter, often threatening punishment and dismissal, this was simply to demonstrate his powerful sway over the lives of his chosen people. They had to observe a specific plan given to them by a good creator for their own well-being. To observe this plan meant reward and blessing. To ignore it, or even to hedge a little, was to invite disaster.

Seeing God as a parental figure, caring, concerned for the good of his children, was a particularly Jewish notion. Contrary to others, the people of God's choice ascribed a certain softness of heart, a kind of divine indulgence to God, even amid repeated failures and bungling on their own part. The all-too-human Jews, who fell into every possible error and shortsighted misstep, were confident of a consistent fidelity from God, who somehow called them back and straightened out their waywardness. Though often depicted as intensely angry, after persuasive pleading by the leaders of the Jewish people, God always "repented" and once again accepted their good resolutions. They were treated as "family," the children of the covenant. A certain sense of "being saved" filled the Jewish spirit, and they looked upon themselves as set apart, above every other nation. God was their God, and they were God's people.

The basis for this complete relationship was always the law, lengthy lists of complex rules, having to do with every possible aspect of daily life. The law applied to even the minutest and remotest dealings. There was nothing which the law did not deal with, from eating, to dress, to obscure forms of ritual and sacrifice. The law came to be all but synonymous with God.

The God of the Old Testament is described in human terms, the best the Jews could do under the circumstances. They had to have some basic framework in which to think. So they pictured God as parent and judge, characterized by anger, patience, wisdom, fidelity to promises, and other human qualities. Those who spoke or wrote about God were attempting to present in simple terms an understandable picture, readily acceptable to the people of that time.

The expression of who God is and the description of how we fit into the plan of creation comes to fullest light in Jesus. This dramatic person arrives on the scene announcing the good news of God's care for us; we are so much more than birds on the wing or flowers in fields. It is the particular gift of Jesus to express in direct and simple terms all that God wants to say to us; that life is good and we have a responsibility for one another, that the very hairs of our heads are numbered, and not even a sparrow falls to the ground without the creator's consent. This good news brings consolation, the courage of confidence in the meaning of our existence; it relaxes many previous fears about God and reassures us of the goodness of life, that we can ask anything in faith and it will be given to us.

This progressive notion of God expressed in Jesus brings a completely new shade of meaning and impact. Whereas in the Old Testament, God was seen as demanding, almost needing the obedience and service of the Jewish people, Jesus speaks of a new order in which the earth, life, and our time here are given to us as a marvelous gift. Through the use of this gift we come to joy, happiness, here and in the time to come. Jesus compares God to an indulgent parent who can embrace a wayward child, even after many sins. He assures us that the greatest commands that God has given have to do with becoming loving people, not only of God, but our neighbor, not only our friends, but our enemies as well, who deserve our regard perhaps even more. That Jesus has come to offer a better and more refined notion of God is obvious in all the gospels. There we find repeated contrasts between the old law and what Jesus has come to say. "You have heard it said . . . but I say to you." This is a recurring phrase used by Jesus to assure his listeners that a momentous change has taken place.

In the early.Christian community, for the first 250 years or so after the death and resurrection of Jesus, God was viewed as deeply personal, entering into the lives of the gathered believers. They remembered what Jesus had said and the extraordinary events which marked his ministry. While there were still some references to God's demands, the unyielding path of justice, and the punishment of unbelievers, generally speaking the notion of God became a welcome part of life. This attitude of optimism and confidence was a basic departure from the fear and misunderstanding of God in previous times.

As the Roman Empire leaned toward Christianity and, finally, when Constantine accepted the Christian faith in 313, the notion of God took on still another dimension. This historic period had truly lasting effects, and many ideas about God which developed at that time have continued down even to our own times.

It began with Roman emperors and gradually affected kings and rulers across the world. These people identified themselves, their power and authority, with the power and authority of God. Somehow, craftily, and with what had to be a certain pragmatism, pushing aside some reasonable objections, the will of the emperor became the will of God. Whatever the emperor said was exactly what God would say. To a lesser or greater extent, God became blurred and was made a partner to, if not completely replaced by, the emperor. This whole issue became so deeply implanted in the minds of the people, they peacefully accepted the incredible principle that whatever the religion of the ruler, that religion automatically became the religion of the people.

Church structure fit rather neatly into such an

attractive setting. This approach guaranteed a high level of obedience and submission to so-called divine authority. A hierarchy was formed in the church, patterned after the structure of the empire, the kingdom. There were marked similarities on both sides, the image of nobility, the triumph of class distinction, and always the continuing assurance of God's approval.

If there were some further inquiries made about God, they were mostly academic, intellectual speculation which didn't call into question the central notion. Augustine, a fifth-century theologian, wrote *The City of God,* a treatise on the order and plan in which everything was in its place and God was the director of all. Thomas Aquinas, a thirteenth century philosopher, wrote much on the subject of God, but mostly from the high chair of reason: Can we prove God's existence? What were the reasons for creation? Is the world as eternal as God? How many angels can dance on the head of a pin? There were others, of course, all competent and brilliant—Anselm, Bonaventure, Cajetan, Albert the Great. But their contribution supported the prevailing notion of God and left it basically unchanged. If anything, God became even more impersonal and rather distant through the work of these enlightened theologians.

So most of us grew up with a fixed idea of how God fit into our lives. It was our vague premonition that many, certainly those in authority, knew God better than we did. Our notions of lord, creator, king, and deity were accepted, handed-down preformed ideas, about which we asked little and assumed much.

In recent years, however, we have begun to see the stirrings of a new awareness of God. We might attribute these stirrings to the simple fact that it is difficult to live with the restrictive ideas of God which developed historically. Whatever the causes, the new awareness began some time ago, took various forms and directions, and just recently began coming to the surface. Obviously, much is changing in our time, hopefully for the better. This new development has not yet run its course, and it will undoubtedly rock back and forth to extreme and middle positions for some time to come. But it is undeniable that change is taking place.

For some, the notion of God has become meaningless in these modern times. The entire effort at trying to discern something of the final meaning of life has become too heavy to bear, asking more questions than it answers, shedding less than satisfying light on life's riddles. This position has been clearly articulated by those who began to write on the subject around the end of the last century. Authors who spent a lot of time thinking and writing about whether life has real significance ended by proposing that what we do here, the efforts we make, are meaningless. In a world in which evil abounds, injustices flourish, dishonesty prevails, and personal integrity is increasingly less visible, it seemed ludicrous to many to talk about God, at least in the terms and descriptions we have used in the past.

It turns out that many people have come to share these feelings. There is too much hardship in people's lives for God to have meaning. Experiences of rejection, hatred, and positive violence have left many with bitter and cynical feelings. For these, there is an acid distaste for Christians who have sometimes been less than sensitive to the needs of those feeling oppression and want. The God proposed by old-time ministers, sung about in standard spirituals, who lets us suffer now but rewards us later, has been discarded in search of something better. To give up on a God who favored only some and disregarded others has been seen as a positive step toward something more purposeful. One hears the strains of "Gimme that old time religion" far less frequently in these days. That sweet chariot which swings low, comin' for to carry us home, is insignificant as compared to a here-and-now satisfaction coming from the assurance that the lion could lie down with the lamb in God's kingdom and that shields could be turned into plows and swords into pruning hooks.

The full repercussions of these ideas and other lines of reasoning are yet to come. But we are seeing much already which might be described as a kind of purging of some mistaken ideas and an attempt to arrive at what seems more reasonable and true.

With the industrial and scientific revolutions, the world began and still continues an unprecedented, radical change. And the whole approach to religion has begun to change with it. Through science and technology, impenetrable mysteries began to give way to probing and understanding. Darkness was replaced with light; the world began to yield many secrets which were thought to be locked inextricably in the labyrinth of eternity. The human family has accomplished more, at least in the technical and scientific sense, in the past one hundred years than since its beginning. Whatever is real and objective has fallen under close scrutiny. Nothing has been overlooked. Life continues to unfold, and nature is yielding its secrets to the relentless thirst for progress and technical advance.

It appears there is nothing which cannot be done, built, understood, called into use, or stored for future reference. The greater the challenge, so much more the resource and resolution to meet it. What will come of all that has happened is yet to be seen.

But an obvious result of this flush of progress is an attitude of unparalleled independence. The need for belief in God, a sense of the Lord of Creation, is much less persuasive now than it was a mere twenty-five years ago.

Answers which satisfied in the past are now refused or viewed as weak and unconvincing. To claim that God constantly intervenes in the world, or that sickness, death, disasters, and tragedies are directly caused by some inscrutable divine plan is viewed by many as immature and faulty reasoning. To attempt to motivate church congregations with the fear of God's punishment is no longer effective. We are looking for more plausible explanations, more reasonable ideas of who God is, leaving off old configurations in search of what is more real and balanced.

Some have declared that God is dead, the issue is closed, and we are now able to move on. This breakdown of belief has come from too many unanswered questions, too much which seems like rationalizing rather than convincing explanation.

Others have simply become agnostic, treating the question as irrelevant. To these people, if God exists, fine; if not, fine again. In the meantime, everyone has to get on with the business of living. So why waste our energies and concerns on something so complex and fruitless?

Then there are those who have given up the active pursuit of knowing God, but retain the deep and solid conviction that their lives have meaning and purpose. They are motivated by an acknowledgment of the worth of every individual, and they are deeply concerned for a better world. These very human people do much toward improving the quality of life and endorse principles of value, giving witness that our opportunities here have significance and meaning. They are inclined to shy away from organized religion, avoid traditional church terminology, but they remain deeply faithful to human commitment.

As one might suspect, there are also those who have remained unaffected by all that has occurred. These have maintained a studied suspicion of anything new, opting for the traditional, disregarding what might cause them to change. They are concerned to preserve what has been handed down from the past, are skeptical of much that is new, and sometimes judge that our trouble started when we began to change. They resist any new notions about God and want to retain what has been passed down. For these people, the idea that God can be fully known, the mystery reduced to complete understanding, is no problem. This position stems from a desire to put God into a manageable frame which avoids dislocating their own security.

There are some who have traded gods, preferring something of the Eastern world with its assurance that God can be found in a philosophy such as pantheism (the belief that everything is divine), or Taoism (a sort of determinism, accepting life the way it is), Nirvana (a quest for that blissful state which guarantees peace in spite of an unpeaceful world), and many others. Who can make a judgment about inclinations such as these? The most one can do is accept sincerity where it happens to be and hope well for those who continue to search.

From this heave and sway, this intense pursuit of a deeper knowledge of that supreme being who gives meaning to existence, many new and healthy initiatives have emerged. It is because people continue to ask relevant questions about God that so much is being said, giving clearer insight into such a difficult subject.

What is new, then, in our approach to God? What can we understand which will assist us in our faith, our desire to grasp the purpose of life through our belief and commitment?

Perhaps of primary importance in contemporary religious thinking is the contention that God is to be found in the world, in our daily lives, our neighbors, and in our work. Contrary to older thinking about God "up there" or off somewhere directing the earthly flow as in some kind of gigantic checker game, theologians are speaking of finding God in every feature of life. Faith in God has to do with cooperating with the purpose of creation, letting God be known by what we are doing for one another, continuing God's work by continuing what has been initiated; it is the direction of parental concern, peace, justice, and sharing life with others as God has shared it with us.

There is a growing conviction among Christians that God's goodness can only be known when we are good to one another; that if we are to experience God's compassion, it has to be from people around us; that God has chosen to diminish evil and suffering in the world as we achieve those ends ourselves. We are the life of God come to the world. We are the image of those qualities which have forever resided in God, the Creator.

In this way, God becomes deeply personal, but not in the distorted sense of exclusive possession, the overworn claim that "I" am one of the limited number of God's chosen friends. It is rather in the sense that we live our lives, walk through the world as it were, leaving evidence of God's presence here because of the way we have lived. The accent here is on life, now, in the world, with the challenge of avoiding isolation, not seeing the world as a tolerable evil because of a heaven to follow. We are beginning to talk more about God's gift of life to us, which implies developing our fullest selves, drawing on our capacities, more fully accepting our human failings.

God is still creating the world through us, and we are personally involved in that effort. What it will finally be is up to us, what we do with the world, how we further its development. We could express this by saying that God is in history through what we are doing. We meet God through the development of our humanity, living life as fully and completely as possible. In this way God is seen to be acting in the world, continuing to create, working toward making life meaningful, revealing love, concern, justice, peace, and goodness, lessening evil, sickness, and even death, and consoling those in sorrow and suffering. But whatever God is accomplishing, it is through us, through what we choose to do. Tc choose positive and productive goals is the total Christian challenge.

Absent, or at least diminished, from our contemporary notion of God is the heavy overlay of fear and impersonalism. Today's direction is away from the God in the distance. It is easier today than a few years ago to know God as warm, personal, knowing and understanding our false starts, the failures in our lives, and with it all, our desires to do better. We have shifted from authority, fear, punishment, wrath, a temperamental and moody God, to assurance, acceptance, partnership, and cooperation.

Obviously, the present age does not have the last word on who God is. No age ever will. There is so much yet to come. There always will be. The worst thing that could befall us would be the naive delusion that we finally know God. We must be content that we know only a little. But what we are saying about all this today seems much more reasonable than what we have sometimes said in the past. If we should abuse the notion of a personal and friendly God by assuming that all this means permissiveness and irresponsibility, we haven't understood. Perhaps this is a necessary shortcoming in the process, something we will yet have to face.

We should hesitate, however, to simply condemn past ideas and efforts to define God. Most people, most times, do the best possible. We're always heir to what goes before us. It is our human privilege to question and to call into doubt. Abuse comes from resisting understanding, knowing but refusing to change, being closed to what is convincing. God is for all times and for all people. The surest reality is that God will survive.

The question, then, must never be so one-sided that it asks only what God has done. It must rather be a question which involves ourselves, and it is better asked from the viewpoint of what we can do to make what God has done become real. This single notion is probably the most significant contribution contemporary theology has made.

There are some things we will never understand. We will always be at a loss to grasp the meaning of certain realities in our lives: the puzzling presence of evil, physical maladies, purposeless and extended sickness, retardation and mental illness, the incomprehensible inequities of life, riches and poverty, the insidious hardness of heart which we seem to develop so easily, the insanity of war, the systematic destruction of so much that is good and beautiful. The list is endless. We can only continue to grapple with these negative aspects of life, know that we can do some things to relieve them, and admit that there is much that we cannot presently understand. As one person expressed it, "God has a lot to answer for." But one thing is certain: there is much that each one of us can do to make God's presence known and felt in the world.

Who, then, is God? This is certainly a question worth asking. The very inquiry itself reveals our conviction that the answer is worth seeking. It indicates our deep and unrelenting need to know something more about our life and our world. It is a question which we have never been able to successfully avoid. Is God dead? Only as dead as we permit. It is possible that all of what God intended to give to the world could be thwarted by our own resistance. Indeed, God could become dead for us. But this is hardly likely. God is already dead for some people. But for many more God is living and acting in our world. God is alive and well.

Chapter 3

Jesus—Who do people say that I am?

The life of Jesus was recently presented on television. The program, directed by Franco Zeferelli, lasted for several weeks. It took an insightful look at who Jesus is as he is described in the gospels. The program was generally well received, with only a few criticisms offered by certain churches and church-related individuals.

I remember talking with a woman in our parish a few days after the last segment. She was commenting on the appeal it held for her, and she concluded with the special reason for her pleasure. "Didn't they pick just the right actor? He looked exactly like Jesus."

I didn't say anything, but in my mind I was asking myself, "Just what does Jesus look like? Who has a picture? How did we get the picture we currently have?" Yet, my friend's response wasn't as meaningless as it might have seemed at first. As a matter of fact, each of us has a personal image of Jesus. It doesn't have much to do with how tall he was, the color of his eyes and hair, or his body build and features. Our pictures go deeper than that. They represent the human qualities which make up the real person rather than the mere physical appearances. In the words of Jesus himself, it's what's inside that counts. We can spend a great deal of energy over what is only skin deep.

Zeferelli's effort is only one among many which add depth to our understanding. We can go to lectures, read books, join discussion groups, get into movements, and even follow active causes which have to do with Jesus. You can find his name on billboards, T-shirts, bumper stickers, and the lips of those who whisper it softly in hushed reverence or sing at the tops of their voices in a rally of thousands. In the past few years we've learned to sing the name, dance to the tune of it, trade reverence toward it for an easier familiarity in the hope of greater closeness. We're constantly asking the question "Who is Jesus?" and we're never quite satisfied with only one answer.

That Jesus was real, lived in the world, went through life the way we do, is all something we accept as true. Why is it so difficult then to know who Jesus was, is? Why must we keep asking the question over and over again? Is it because the question is so broad? Is it because the answers to the questions pose more questions about ourselves? If we know who Jesus is, does that imply something momentous and singular in our own lives? Have we avoided some things in Jesus because we'd rather not live with what he is really saying to us?

The traditional teaching of the church sees Jesus as a human person, yet not quite human, as we are. Even though we have never denied the humanity of Jesus, we haven't really emphasized it either. It has always been easier for us to talk about his divinity, to speak of him as God. So we have surrounded Jesus with God-like qualities and enriched that tradition to such an extent that we have lost sight of his human nature. Any time you ask a grade school child, and many older people, who Jesus is, the unvarying answer is that he is God. The answer is only half true and, in itself, leaves a most

important part of the question unanswered. If Jesus
came to speak to us of God, to show us how to live, his appeal comes from the fact that he is human. If he were
only God, or even more divine than human, it would be difficult if not impossible for us to relate what he had to say
to our own lives, to the daily limitations which our
very human nature places upon us. If Jesus didn't struggle, experience the same kinds of agony and ecstacy we
do, feel intense human emotion and the unavoidable
weaknesses of the human character, then he really
wouldn't be touching our lives. We could go so far as to
say that God didn't really speak to us on our level.

This tradition of overlooking the humanity of Jesus
began in the earliest church, in fact with the writers of
the gospels themselves. It is understandable that the
early Christian community wanted to portray him in the
most convincing possible light. It was natural to speak
of him in terms of impact, heroic deeds, arresting per-
sonality. The gospels speak of the miraculous circumstances of his birth, his early genius in speaking to the
Pharisees and teachers in the temple, the spirit of dignity
and sureness with which he approached his work. We are
fascinated by the miracles which Jesus performed, the
hearts he transformed, the generous abandon with which
he accepted any and all people. We tend to forget that he
was tired, hungry, afraid, sometimes fiercely angry, frustrated, confused, joyful, laughing, confident, and that he
experienced the same emotions, the same highs and lows
which we do.

Even though a lot of time has been spent in defending
the humanity of Jesus, it might be said that we have had
our fingers crossed. The vocabulary used to express who
Jesus was strongly suggests that we are again more concerned about his divinity than his humanity. Theologians
have spoken of Jesus' knowledge of the divine will,
the ever-present face of God, a sort of permanent beatif-
ic vision, a rapture which assisted Jesus, even though
human, to gracefully move through life without the

extensive efforts which we must exert. They have talked about his marvelous interior qualities, a conscious divine setting from which he operated.

This is the background out of which most of us, certainly most Catholics, have come. It is asking a lot of ourselves to relinquish any or all of that, to move into renewal where Jesus is concerned.

The Jesus of tradition and doctrine has endured for centuries. It is only in recent times that people are beginning to question that image for our real, everyday lives. We have begun to ask what might seem to be irreverent questions, to face issues which have always raised holy eyebrows in the past. What good is it for us if Jesus was mostly God with just a little mixture of humanity? Did Jesus even know he was God, or simply have a notion of holy mission, a premonition of calling which he saw fit to follow with a deep sense of courage? What is truly important about Jesus? His power, authority, dignity? Or is it his likeness to us and his intense desire for us to know that God cares for us? What is important for Jesus? To show us what God can do or to speak to us of what God has done for us? Are we to approach Jesus with a genuflection of awe and fear, or rather with the confidence of companionship toward someone who comes as friend, taking our part and doing it with us?

These questions are not only asked by theologians but by people from every walk of life. Many times the questions have been asked more clearly, more incisively by those who are not theologians. Can Jesus be real, saddened by the foolishness of Judas? Can he actually be afraid to die on that fearful night, crying out, "Take me now before I change my mind?" Is there a possibility that Jesus was a friend and companion to women, loved with the heart? Could he cry in genuine agony, in complete lack of understanding, feeling utter destitution as he died, perhaps wondering to what purpose? These are the questions to which millions have sung and danced across the world in *Jesus Christ, Superstar.* The questions themselves are of such unprecedented depth and magnitude that they can only be sung out, treated almost as fiction, but always with that shade of absolute sincerity and with a demand to be answered.

The questions are asked again in *Godspell*. Can Jesus be so personally attractive through his innocence, so guileless that he can beguile the hardest hearts? What is the meaning of life? Did we miss a turn somewhere, and has Jesus come to help us get back? Do we begin by turning cheeks, helping the helpless, being wise enough to put up with the foolishness of life, settling for what is small, which turns out to be far greater than we had anticipated?

The questions are not new. But they have never been asked with such serious regard, with such intense hope of better answers. They are born out of a consciousness of too much which is awry, too much which is left undone in today's Christian world. After two thousand years there are many who have never received the message of hope and peace. Those who have received it often find it garbled and inapplicable in a world of stress and fracture. Has God truly come into the world as one of us, or must we still wait? Did Jesus want to show the world that human nature is capable of unbelievable accomplishments?

There is an obvious difference between living life with Jesus and asking him to live it for us. If Jesus came to tell us about taking up our cross and doing our part, it wasn't to take life away from us but rather to give it to us more richly. It isn't so much a matter of admiring how Jesus lived life, as receiving the message that what he has done, we must go and do likewise.

We have no assurance that Jesus will take our hand and lead us through life as though we had no input, nothing to contribute. In recent years, many people have developed a "leave it to Jesus" attitude in which they rely on the heavy assistance of immediate intervention. We hear phrases such as "The Lord told me to do it," or "and then I was led by the Lord." This sort of mentality implies that Jesus is whispering in our ear, telling us when and how, letting us exist in a state of paralysis until we get the signal from him. There is little if anything to substantiate such an interaction between Jesus and us. He rather speaks of the Christian life in terms of accepting the mission which has already been announced to us. Jesus doesn't solve our problems. We do. We solve them because God has been good enough to give us the necessary resources to cope with whatever life offers. Jesus has come to announce this and to show us that the human person is quite capable of accepting such a challenge and living life to the full.

Seeing Jesus as an almighty problem solver, saving us from drugs, sin, foolhardy decisions, and bad companions leaves us with too little of God's assurance that it is good to be human and that Jesus was human. This way we would simply be clothing the traditional doctrines about Jesus with the same garments of divinity over humanity.

The real Jesus is extremely difficult to face, even threatening. Most of us would rather settle for traditional notions about him than accept the challenge of doing what he did. We are suffering from the same discomfort as the people who were contemporaries of Jesus. They found what he said entirely unacceptable, out of mesh with their beliefs. Jesus had a particularly sharp sensitivity for seeing through rationalizations, false dignity, and the sanctity of the law for law's sake. He was courageous enough to criticize religious leaders and ridicule their inaction. He chose friends among sinners and derelicts rather than important people. He was angry enough to call the church structure a sham and a hypocrisy. He talked about the real issues in a way that was completely different from what had been taught: the importance of love over the letter of the law, forgiveness over authority and power, service rather than being served, kindness enough to give bread not a stone, and an egg not a scorpion.

Against such a background, the questions which theologians are asking about Jesus today are important indeed. Are we avoiding issues also? Are we believing in doctrines and traditional teachings about Jesus rather than facing what is true about him, that he was human just as we and that he doesn't expect any more from us than he did from himself? Is it easier to concentrate on elaborate ecclesiastical structure, laws and doctrine, lavish church buildings, intricate steps in Christian conversion, rejection of other churches on the basis of unsound doctrine? Does paying too much attention to these conditions take us away from Jesus, his message, the great commandments of love of God and neighbor?

Where would you find Jesus in today's society? The answer to that question should give a clearer indication of where we should find ourselves in living out the Christian life. What lifestyle would Jesus be embracing? Where would he be living? In what part of the city? What kind of car would he drive? Who would his friends be, and would he limit his friendship to just certain persons? What books would he be reading, what television and movies would he be watching? If these questions seem far-fetched, out of focus, is it because we have relegated Jesus to a theological corner where he doesn't have too much effect on our modern lives? Has past theology put Jesus in church buildings, in devotion to a name which has come to indicate not a person but rather an idea?

There are more questions. How would Jesus speak in today's society? How would he approach the many problems which come up, which we always hope will go away, but never do? Would he have some judgments about war? What would he have to say about nuclear weapons and the possible destruction of the entire world? What about the poverty and destitution which paralyze the lives of so many good people? Would Jesus say anything about the systematic destruction of the environment or the depletion of resources by a few privileged nations in the world? Would Jesus be a politician? What would he have to say about the greed and theft in our time, about multinational corporations?

Would Jesus be as hard on us as we sometimes are on ourselves? Would the same Jesus who spoke of the generous father of the prodigal son be as unforgiving of sinners as we sometimes are, filled with resentment and prejudice? Could we expect him to be less understanding, less sensitive toward sinners, the adultress, the tax collector, than he originally was? Would he refuse to associate with those who are married "out of the church"? Would he be concerned about long and complex lists of laws about who is worthy to be called a Catholic, who may receive communion, when confession is valid, and whether babies go to Limbo because they haven't been baptized?

Obviously, we can't know the exact answers to many of these questions. But we gain some convincing indications in the gospels. Those indications point to the fact that we might have wasted a lot of time on issues which have less relevance than we had originally thought. Even though we can't have all the answers, it is the business of theology to keep us honest, straight in our thinking. It is easy to go off in the wrong direction and concern ourselves with doctrine and tradition to the loss of the real and human person of Jesus.

It is the work of theology to continue the process of knowing more and more about God's dealings with us. Specifically, how God's work is accomplished in Jesus. That work revolves around always trying to know the truth. Such work is reasonable, not irreverent, nor simply looking for change for its own sake. Theology should always bring life to religion, not make it more difficult. Sometimes in the past, and even in the present, some theologians and those who are in authority have used theology for control and manipulation. To ask for a change is healthy.

What are some of the changes which have taken place about Jesus? For one, we are talking more about Jesus as a common, ordinary person like ourselves. This isn't to take away his dignity, his nobility, but to acknowledge that his very greatness, his true dignity and nobility, come from the fact that he was human and yet was able to live his life with such fullness and accomplishment. That gives us a lot of hope. It helps us to identify with him. So we are seeing something new in Jesus, not new of itself, but new to us. In the past, we used a variety of titles in referring to Jesus: King, Master, Messiah, Lord. The exclusive use of these titles takes us away from some very important aspects of Jesus. They emphasize what is different about him, rather than how he is like us. It's interesting to note that Jesus never referred to himself by these titles. They were rather picked up by the church along the way. This is not to blame the church for wanting to identify the greatness of Jesus; it is simply in the interest of accuracy. Jesus didn't talk very much about himself. When he did, it was always pointing to something larger which he wanted to say. There wasn't much egotism in him. It's a point worth making because we sometimes have a tendency to assume that Jesus thought he was very important, which isn't the case at all. Such knowledge helps us to realize that we should be concerned less for pleasing Jesus by giving him big titles and more for responding to what he said, doing what he did. One suspects that if you asked him which was more important, to use the title "Christ the King" or to try to live out all those things he said in the Sermon on the Mount, the answer would be obvious.

Perhaps we can begin to see that we are not talking so much about change in our belief or attitude toward Jesus, but simply remembering some aspects about him which we might have forgotten over the years. It is remarkable that Jesus talked so little about rules and regulations. It is remarkable because in our time in the church, there are so many rules, we have to have a large book called Canon Law, or the Code of Canon Law, to contain all of them. In the time of Jesus, the Pharisees and scribes saw their job as interpreters of the law. If you had a question to ask, or sometimes even if you didn't ask, these experts could quote the law and its minutest applications. The rules of living in that time were called the Mosaic law. There were 613 of them, each with a lot of footnotes and additions. In the Catholic church, there are 2,414 laws, each with its own set of footnotes and additions.

The paradox of all this, the truth we may have forgotten, is that Jesus came to tell us that the law is far less important than the person. He indicated that slavish obedience to the law could take you so far away from the purpose of life that the law could become a god in itself. St. Paul understood what Jesus was saying, and he later declared that the law could take away our life. We know that Paul was telling the truth because we are quite capable of being thoroughly law-abiding and, at the same time, not really good persons.

So in recent years the church is trying to emphasize that aspect of Jesus in which he was less concerned about rules and regulations and more concerned about personal conversion of heart and mind. The church is not saying that laws are unimportant; it is saying that Jesus called us to progress beyond the letter of the law to the spirit and the value which the law represents and expresses.

Another change in our approach to Jesus has to do with our own response to what he said to us. Jesus came calling for conversion, a personal change of heart away from what is mediocre and second best in us. He came to say that we could do better than we had been doing. This doesn't mean that we should be neurotic about the Christian life, treat it as though it were a win-or-lose game in which God had the advantage. But it does mean that we are asked to respond to the invitation of Jesus to change the world. To believe in Jesus calls for change, change which is always taking place, renewing itself. Belief in Jesus doesn't mean belief that Jesus has done it all, that we can sit back, say a few prayers, get in our "obligations," and expect everything to happen. It means that we accept his challenge to change the world, and to know it can be done because he did it first. At the beginning of his public life, Jesus said to the people: "Repent, for the kingdom of God is here." We ordinarily think that repentance implies being sorry for our sins, being able to admit our faults and do something about them. But there is a deeper meaning to the word. It has to do with making whatever changes are necessary to make room for a new reality in our lives. If that change means that we have to admit our faults, fine. But it might simply mean that we should grow in appreciation of the worth of something. In the case of the kingdom of God, Jesus is simply assuring us that there are some things we have to do. Once we understand what they are, whatever changes are necessary to do them will come naturally.

We must ask what changes we can make in our attitude toward Jesus which might help us to understand better the meaning of the Christian life. That consideration should include an understanding of what Jesus came to do. He came to tell us that many of the things we thought were awfully important actually weren't important at all. On the other hand, what we have thought unimportant suddenly becomes essential. There are endless examples of all this in the gospels, in what Jesus said. Highest among these important realities is the forgiveness of sin and acceptance of people, no matter who or how bad they are. So in order to exemplify this principle, Jesus forgives and reassures prostitutes, tax collectors, an adulteress, religious fanatics, anybody who comes along. He not only forgives people, but he keeps insisting that this is exactly the attitude of God toward us. He keeps telling us that God is like our parent, just as indulgent, accepting, and even willing to appear foolish with affection for us.

There are other features of Jesus important to consider. He talked in what seemed riddles and paradoxes. Just when you'd expect him to say one thing, he'd say another, entirely different. Instead of saying it was better to be first, he said being last was best. He insisted that we find life when we lose it. He told us we can never hold grudges against others, not even our worst enemies. He talked in terms of peace and non-resistance in the face of anger and persecution.

Obviously, many people in the time of Jesus couldn't live with such thinking. They were deeply involved in a long-standing tradition which made them feel secure and right. They had already settled many of the problems Jesus was addressing. They felt they knew God better than he did. Hadn't they been working on all this for centuries? Didn't they have precedence because they had developed a long-standing tradition? Wasn't Jesus a newcomer to the scene?

Jesus didn't worry about authority, about the hierarchy of his day. This is another aspect about him which we might have forgotten. As a matter of fact, he positively discouraged the people of his time from following the example of the scribes and Pharisees. He said that what they were requiring was too complex. There were too many rules. He said it was better to be like a little child.

It is good to remember that Jesus always gave a convincing illustration of what he was saying. He said that we shouldn't worry about what to eat or wear. As a persuasive proof of all that, he lived very simply. He claimed that peacemakers would be blessed and then offered no resistance when he was arrested, tried, and executed. Jesus did very little theorizing and was much more concerned with how life should be lived.

Jesus came assuring us that we could live meaningfully, make a contribution, and have good feelings about ourselves even though we fall short of the ideal; and we should never settle for the notion that religion belongs to the elect, and not to everybody. If Jesus said all that, and he certainly did, why do we keep insisting that only a few people are truly good? Why is it so difficult to see the good in one another, so much easier to concentrate on our faults, or better, the faults of others? Just about anyone will admit that we certainly need some changes in this regard. Perhaps the most important change begins in ourselves and has to do with being satisfied that we are human, knowing that this is all that is expected of us.

Are we changing our attitude toward Jesus? Is theology about Jesus shifting to a less rigid approach? Perhaps we are just returning to what existed in the early church, a confident approach to the person of Jesus who assures us that he has come in our behalf to tell us that God accepts us.

Jesus said that the kingdom of God was like finding a treasure in a field; that once we find it, we are so convinced of its value, we are willing to sell everything we have to obtain it. That might initially mean some discomfort. But it offers eventual satisfaction. Such satisfaction demands the element of risk, a leap outside of security and comfort toward the struggle which in itself gives peace.

Chapter 4

Scripture

If our age will be noted for some remarkable break-throughs, one of them will be the affirmation of the need for communication. It is common to hear people say we need to communicate more, dialogue, discuss, and inter-relate. We often say that it is impossible to isolate our-selves and to refuse to talk with others. We even maintain that without communication we might as well not be alive. Sometimes we hear about parents who lock their children in dark rooms or treat them in some inhuman way. This horrifies us and evokes a compassion in us for anyone who would be treated this way. We would like to deny the privilege of parenthood to those who do not ap-preciate the basic need to communicate with those who depend on them. Sometimes we read statistics about how little real communication takes place within so-called normal families. We hear how very little time is spent in real conversation among family members. It frightens us because we know, at least theoretically, how extremely important dialogue and communication are.

A modern expression we often use to refer to our relationship with God has to do with being children and family of God, who is our good and caring parent. In using such an expression, we wish to signify that God is everything and more than parents should be, mother and father to us all. We believe in God's care for us and trust that we will receive whatever we need for our well-being.

At the same time, we reason that God expects certain responses from each of us, just as human parents expect certain responses from their children. We take it for granted that God has a right to make such demands as the giver and keeper of life.

If all of this is true, and it seems reasonable that it is, there are some conclusions we could draw about God as our parent and ourselves as his children. First of all, we should be able to expect that God would speak to us in some way, telling us some things about ourselves which we wouldn't know otherwise, reassuring us about who we are and what our purpose is. Then, if God is demanding something from us, we could expect that whatever it is should be communicated to us in some way. Otherwise it would be difficult, if not impossible, to know about God and ourselves, what our place is here, and what we can expect from life and the future.

So we are expressing a legitimate question when we ask how God speaks to us and what he is saying. If God always accomplishes good, and we believe this is true, we deserve to receive whatever messages are necessary for that purpose.

But how does God communicate? We can answer that question with at least some satisfaction by saying that God is always speaking to us, in people, in circumstances around us, even in our thinking and dreaming. We can be sure that just as parents speak to their children, God, our parent, speaks to us with equal interest and concern.

As Christians, we believe that there is an even more specific and comforting response to the question of how God communicates with us. We believe that the Scripture, the Bible, is the most obvious and significant medium God uses to communicate. We say that Scripture is the Word of God. We could say that Scripture is the word which is composed of many words to give one message: that God wants to offer us a guide for living, to express interest and concern, and to assure us there is meaning and purpose to our lives.

Scripture, the Bible, is divided into two major sections, the Old Testament and the New Testament. The Old Testament records those significant events in the relationship of the Jewish people to God up to the time of Jesus. The New Testament presents the life and actions of Jesus and all those events which followed after his time in the establishment of the early church. Hardly anyone has ever contended that the Scriptures are God's only communication with the world, but most of us maintain that they are the major and most important expression to us. So we place a great deal of emphasis on them and are always studying them, looking deeper into their meaning, and wanting to discover the fuller sense of what they say.

Most Christians hold that the Scriptures are inspired. In simple terms, inspiration means that whoever wrote the Scriptures was at least unconsciously getting the message correct with no possibility of error. This doesn't mean to say that the writers knew they were being inspired, as though God were whispering in their ear or was taking their hand and guiding the pen. It has more to do with our assurance that if God is going to take the trouble to speak to us, we can be sure the message will be reliable and true. Most good scripture scholars teach that inspiration has much more to do with the total message than with the details surrounding it. For example, the Book of Genesis records how God appeared to Moses in a burning bush. If in fact the bush turned out to be a tree or a large rock, we shouldn't become upset as though that detail would change the fact that God "appeared" in some way to Moses. The substance of the message remains the same. The truth that God sometimes speaks to us in very special ways remains intact.

It is readily understandable that something as important as the Scriptures could easily become the subject of intense controversy. First of all, someone might be tempted to say that we know exactly what God is saying in the Bible and there is no further need to look for deeper meanings. Some Christians hold that we should take the Scriptures literally, as though each word has its own special significance, and any new thoughts or changes invariably damage what was originally intended. For these people, details are very important. Literal interpretation is a must. If the Bible says that God created the world in seven days, it means just that, seven twenty-four-hour periods, seven risings and seven settings of the sun. If the Scriptures say that Noah took two of every living creature on the ark, interpretation must be literal, two elephants and two gnats, two lions and two lambs.

Today, many people criticize this literal approach. They say, first of all, that such slavish obedience to details might confuse the real message. If we ardently believe the story of the ark with all its details and skip over the deep truth that God disapproves of and punishes sinful people, we have missed the communication that the Bible is offering us. If God speaks to us the way we speak to one another, then we can be confident that details are less important than the truth of the message itself.

Those who interpret the Bible literally are sometimes criticized for their lack of awareness of how the Scriptures came into existence. They presume they were written immediately when or at least shortly after the events occurred. Take the example of the burning bush again. One could mistakenly assume that Moses went home after his vision and wrote everything in a book where he was keeping a record of such things. But there is too much evidence that this was not the case. As a matter of fact, the Scriptures developed from oral tradition. What that means is this: the faith of the early Jewish people was handed down not in writing, but by word of mouth, from one generation to another. This passing on of stories and belief went from parents to children who became parents and handed them on to their own children. Eventually they were written down, but not from the beginning. As a matter of fact, oral tradition was sometimes hundreds of years old before it was put down in written form.

What all this means is that it is quite possible that details and minute circumstances could have been changed or confused in their passing. Again it is easier to believe that the substance of the message handed down remained intact even if the wording or order changed. If inspiration means God guarantees that the whole message is true, we do no damage to Scripture by holding that some aspects are more important than others. It is more important to know that somehow our nature has been injured than to know what kind of fruit Adam and Eve ate or where the garden of Eden was. Believing that God protected and nurtured the chosen people is much more important than getting caught in the details of how Samson slew thousands of Philistines with the jawbone of an ass.

No one has said that we could not believe in these lesser circumstances of Scripture. If we choose to do so, we may. But for many it simply seems unreasonable to demand such strict submission to what appears unimportant. It would be foolish to say that one could not be a good and believing Christian unless a literal interpretation were accepted. Such an approach is too unscientific for many sincere people. As we have said, literalism sometimes gets us away from the real meaning of the message.

What is said of the Old Testament can be said with equal confidence of the New Testament. It is true, however, that the life and deeds of Jesus were written soon after his death and resurrection. But even the New Testament is based on the oral tradition which preceded what was written about Jesus and the early church. We know that the earliest gospel, that of Mark, was not written until several decades after the death of Jesus. The other gospels and writings followed at even later times.

It is again evident that there is a message in the entire New Testament which is more important than individual details. We can add to this the fact that the twenty-seven books of the New Testament should be considered together, as a whole, rather than laying stress on any individual work. It is by reading and digesting them all that we get a clear picture of who Jesus was and how the early church came to be. Individual evangelists and writers place different emphases on particular features of Jesus and those early years of Christianity. But the substance of the message is clear: Jesus came speaking the word of God and encouraging us to respond to an invitation to accept the kingdom God had prepared for us.

By now it should be clear that those who oppose a literal interpretation of the Scriptures are looking more at the meaning, and they are not insisting that every word of Scripture must be taken as essential. These people do not ask what each word is saying but rather what God wants to reveal to us through the stories or events which are taking place. They would not be upset if it became undeniably apparent that Jonah didn't actually live in the stomach of a whale for several days. They would be more interested in the message that we must offer God our obedience and submission when it is asked of us and that God will not be put off. They believe there is a meaning which goes beyond the story of the event which is recorded, something that is being specifically revealed as God's way of communicating to us.

For those who prefer this deeper and fuller sense, Scripture offers an expression of God's concern and solicitude rather than a rigid demand that we believe without question or study. The Scriptures contain messages of comfort and reassurance. God is good, and he has created us as an affirmation of that goodness. We have not always appreciated what God has accomplished for us, and we have sometimes missed the message. But God keeps calling us back by renewing covenants and promises with us. He keeps repeating this through important persons, leaders and prophets, holy men and women, who express the message in various ways, keeping us in tune. And he reminds us to the fullest and clearest degree in the person of Jesus, the Word who comes saying that it is all so.

Whether we insist on a literal interpretation of Scripture or opt for seeing the message in events and stories, interpreting the inspired Word of God cannot be a matter of rugged individualism. The Scriptures are obviously complex. They were written long ago, in obscure languages, and by people who had a different notion of how history should be recorded. We do not possess any of the original writings and must rely on copies which are hundreds of years removed from the actual authors. Most of us have to depend on translations which have been worded in ways which make the original Scriptures more understandable. There are dozens of different translations. One need only compare any two to see how the words and even the details differ.

Persons of high intellectual ability have made the Scriptures their life study. They have learned the original languages, returned to the actual setting of many of the events of the Bible, pored over and compared sometimes minute details of a single passage. It is far better to rely on their interpretation than our own in matters of difficulty. This does not mean that we should not read the Scriptures, we should encourage one another to do so. It does not mean that we cannot understand them. Much of Scripture is plainly written. It simply means that the fuller study of the Bible has become a science which requires background and insight. Sometimes the interpretation of those who are qualified makes what seemed difficult much clearer. A simple commentary on what a word or phrase in the original language means helps much more than relying on our own sense of what they might say. One of the distinct blessings of our times is that we do have clear and well worded translations which assist us tremendously in understanding the Bible. These improvements are the gift of interested scholars who want to add to our appreciation and enlightenment.

We might reasonably ask how we came to have the books we do in the Bible, why forty-five in the Old Testament and twenty-seven in the New Testament? Obviously, there were other writings. As a matter of fact, there were many others. Furthermore, the church didn't settle on the selection of specific writings until some time after the first century. The criteria used were these. First, the works were accepted on the basis that they were widely used by the early church communities. Secondly, they were looked upon as expressing those truths which were in keeping with the faith which was believed and practiced by the people. It might seem that one or another legitimate work could have been missed in that manner of selection or that something could have slipped in which shouldn't be there. But we can reasonably depend on the truth of what is contained in the Scriptures and reaffirm our own belief that they are inspired, which is to say that God's message and communication to us are surely contained there.

Clearly, most Christians have come to view some of the works of Scripture as more important than others. Clearly also, some of the works have less application to our lives. Reading the Book of Numbers for example, about the actual count of Jewish tribes and people, is not very stimulating. In Leviticus and Deuteronomy, various complex laws are related which have no meaning for our time. It is not irreverent to say that the time spent reading the Scriptures could be better spent on more relevant material found in other parts of the Bible.

Sometimes Scripture is highly colored with the writing style of the time in which it was written. Some works are allegorical, containing messages within stories and extended metaphors. Others are proverbial, simply stating principles and wise sayings. Again, deeper truths and meanings should be sought.

In the New Testament the Book of Revelation causes particular difficulty for many people who read it. It is clearly prophetic, predicting future events and their bearing on the church. There might be a tendency to be overzealous in interpreting what is said there as applied to modern times, singling out communism as the personification of the devil or seeing events in our time heralding the end of the world, or gaining assurance there that one is destined for rapture and salvation while many who believe differently will certainly be condemned. Qualified scripture scholars maintain that it is much saner to see the message as applicable in terms of the struggle of good and evil in each of us and not blaming others for what is clearly the fault of us all. Rather than concentrating on hidden conspiracies and uncontrollable evil forces in the world, we should perhaps be willing to do more ourselves by way of good works after the example of Jesus. It does little good to wring our hands and wait for the end.

In our study and appreciation of the Scriptures, we might miss the notion that they are not only to be read and relished as beautiful, but they are to be lived. We sometimes say that we are called to "preach the word of God." Jesus said simply that not just saying, "Lord, Lord" qualifies us for entrance into the kingdom, but hearing and then doing what the Bible says is required. It is true that the Scriptures must be reverenced, seen as a medium of God's presence to us. But hearing the word, we are called to keep it by what we do and say in representing the message to our time. The word *evangelize* is a word for all seasons which should mean that we are making God's Word known to those around us and even to the far reaches of the world. Making the Word known implies action and living in such a way as to convince others that what we have heard has deep meaning and our lives have changed because of it.

In recent times we have witnessed a tendency to use the Bible for the purpose of proving points and winning arguments. Perhaps this has always been the case, but there seems to be a sometimes careless use of what the Scriptures are saying. Sometimes we abuse what is being said in our zeal to prove a point. We can prove almost anything we like by drawing some passage, sometimes completely out of context, as if it were specifically applicable to our line of reasoning. We sometimes use the same passage to prove opposite views. We are even tempted to interpret the mind of God as though we had some special insight into what is being said.

The Scriptures are meant to encourage, inspire, and reveal God's care for us. They are only secondarily meant to be strong bases for arguments and proving points. We would do well to use them more prudently and always with an effort to see their value for affirming that what God is saying in our lives has meaning and purpose.

The study of Scripture is never finished. It would be foolish to think that we could know all there is to know about the Bible. Just as we cannot know God completely, neither can we know the fullness of revelation. God is always revealing new realities in our lives in many ways. One of them is through the Scriptures which are always new and constantly opening new insights, even though we have studied them for centuries.

Many theologians teach that if Jesus were truly human, like us in all things, it is reasonable to say that he only came to know himself gradually, the way each of us does. They maintain that he had no previous knowledge, no miraculous insight. He grew in age and wisdom. This would imply that his awareness increased with age, came to fuller light. Jesus, according to modern theology, never stopped learning. Even at the end of his life there was still some confusion and doubt. The gospels very strongly suggest that this is the case. Jesus struggled until the end.

We might say that our awareness of the Scriptures

is somewhat similar to the life of Jesus. Just as there was a gradual awakening and discovery and learning in his life, so the Scriptures are always a source of new understanding for us. As we study them, we grow with them as it were, so that we are always coming to fuller life and more awareness. We keep discovering realities and thoughts we might have missed before. Sometimes we experience such sudden awakening it almost seems miraculous. We might read a passage or chapter we have read many times before; but this time we catch something we had never thought of, something which seems entirely new.

But just as Jesus struggled to know who he was and what his mission might be, we struggle in a similar way with the Scriptures. Just as Jesus was human, so the Scriptures can in a sense be said to be equally human, not meant to answer all questions, solve all difficulties, and take all the risk out of life. They rather provide one more insight into God—expressing his care and meaningful concern for us. They assure us that our relationship to God has purpose and that it is worth our effort to make that relationship a real priority in our lives. The Scriptures tell us that many people have gone before us, living meaningfully, being aware of others, and accomplishing good because they believed. They indicate that God assists us and encourages us to meet life head on.

It is true, then, that we understand the Scriptures better when we struggle to grasp their meaning, which is sometimes difficult to perceive. Sometimes they leave us confused and frustrated, even though we study them thoroughly. But they are not meant to discourage us or make us feel we will never make any headway. They certainly are not the restricted territory of the scripture scholars who are supposed to have the wisdom to tell us what the Bible is saying, as though we could never learn anything on our own.

Perhaps the best way to approach Scripture is with a discussion group, listening to what each person has to contribute and reaching some consensus through the group. There is certainly no need to be afraid of Scripture as though there were cryptic and mysterious revelations there meant for only a few.

Sometimes when we are reflecting on how our lives have been meaningful, what we have accomplished, we feel a flush of gratitude toward those who have assisted us. We feel happy that we have had good encounters with people, with our parents. We are grateful for what they have taught us, that they have instilled sound values in us which last and continue to bring good to our daily lives. We appreciate the time spent in communication, their expressions of care and solicitude for us.

There is surely something of that same feeling in our reflections about Scripture, God's expression of his care and solicitude in our regard. We might reflect at times how God has done great things for us and certainly was not obliged to go to such lengths to express such concern. The fact that God's expression of kindness and parental care can be so readily perceived in Scripture should be a source of comfort and peace to us. The Scriptures are one in a series of many gestures from God that are given to assure us that there is a voice, a spirit among us which calls us to be family members where speaking and listening are natural and can be gracefully expected.

Chapter 5

Authority

"Do you promise to me and my successor obedience and reverence?" "I promise." With that exchange in the ordination ceremony, the bishop admits the newly ordained priest into a structure which traditionally assumed that he would be wholly submissive, obedient without question, and completely uncritical. In the attitude of the church, he has become the exclusive possession of a bishop or religious superior who would be the voice of authority, the approved and appointed representative of God's will for him.

In the past, the newly ordained priest was assigned without consultation, and most often without conscious acknowledgment of any particular gifts he might have. It was not unusual that his first assignment would last for years. His future was wholly directed by the bishop or superior, regardless of circumstances which were sometimes oppressive and subject to the judgment of those over him.

Superiors rarely admitted that those under their authority could be more intelligent or gifted than they were.

It was assumed that decisions, demands, and inconsistencies in some superiors were to be accepted without question, on the basis of the structure which had prevailed from the beginning. Whoever wished to participate had to pay the price of quiet acceptance. The future was viewed in terms of being obedient now, with a view toward eventual promotion to a state of gradual independence.

Anyone who took part in the structure had to deal with the written and unwritten demands of superiors. All people in religious life, priests, sisters, and brothers, were clearly advised that certain requirements could be made of them because of the dignity and sacred character of the kind of life they were embracing. The value of such a state was well worth giving up family ties, personal property, eating in public, privacy, questioning of one's superior, and many other "sacrifices." Entire books, called "Rules of Order," were written to explain the meaning of religious life.

The sometimes forgotten body of lay people, the masses of people who regularly filled the pews at Sunday Mass, were not entirely spared this complicated scheme of command and obedience. It was inevitable that such a well developed structure of authority would be assimilated into the life of every member of the church. The church assumed to itself the power of passing judgment on everything "religious" in the lives of its people: marriage and the sacraments, laws and legal effects, qualities necessary for membership, conditions of incorporation, and the right to expel members at any time for various shortcomings.

To begin with, we should define the term *authority*. In *Webster's Collegiate Dictionary,* it is described as "the capacity to influence thought or behavior; the granting of freedom toward a given act; the power or right to give commands, enforce obedience, take actions, or make final decisions." Obedience is natural when the demand is reasonable. We obey because we understand the reason for obedience. To obey blindly for the sake of the command itself is not a virtue at all, but a slavish submission from fear of punishment. Real authority, the kind which should prevail in the church, should be undeniably clear to the person obeying. If clarity cannot be demonstrated, obedience should not be asked.

We can get a good idea of authority in the church from what Jesus had to say about it. It becomes even clearer when we look at certain contrasts which gradually developed in the later church.

When theologians today speak of authority, most of them begin with the incredible action of Jesus washing the feet of the apostles at the Last Supper.

He picked up a towel and tied it around himself. Then he poured water into a basin and began to wash his disciples' feet and dry them with the towel he had around him. . . . After he had washed their feet, he put his cloak back on and reclined at table once more. He said to them: "Do you understand what I just did for you? . . . What I just did was to give you an example; as I have done, so you must do. I solemnly assure you, no slave is greater than his master; no messenger outranks the one who sent him. Once you know all these things, blest will you be if you put them into practice." (John 13:4-17)

Here is a clear indication of what Jesus considers to be of tremendous importance among the apostles and disciples. That importance is obvious in the early community of believers. These people are deeply concerned for one another as described in the Acts of the Apostles. If someone is in need, the rest of the community responds with sensitive awareness. Those who have more, give to those who have less. The Christian group is characterized by its willingness to distribute equally all that they possess. St. Paul mentions this notion often while exhorting the people to serve one another. St. James points out the importance of caring for those who are in need. In all these instances, the ideas of serving, caring for one another, accepting the opportunity of "washing one another's feet," are clearly emphasized over the importance of commands and obedience.

By contrast, then, the movement away from service and concern into the area of authority and submission can readily be seen as an early development in the church. By the time of the Inquisition, for example, concern for the individual had diminished. Historians have a tendency to make too much of this period, painting a picture of rampant terror and torture. Insight would reveal that the majority of Christians were untouched by what happened at this time in the church. But to keep the record true, it did affect the lives of many, some with unbelievable hardship. In the interests of strict orthodoxy, in the interests of what we sometimes call "doctrinal purity," accusations of heresy and nonbelief were prevalent. The punishment for such aberations ranged from banishment to death.

Another contrast can be cited. People were attracted to Jesus because he gave much and asked little. This was clear in his approach to sinners. On one occasion a woman who had been caught in adultery was brought before Jesus. The scribes and Pharisees wanted to stone her, which was the usual punishment for such an act. Jesus advocated leniency and indicated that we all sin. In the end he forgave the woman and simply urged her not to sin anymore.

From the earliest times, adultery was considered unforgivable. The church has spoken nowhere with greater "authority" than in the area not only of adultery, but the entire spectrum of sex. Books, endless commentaries, moral frames, and the minutest laws have been written about the topic. Nothing has been left for speculation; there has not been the slightest admission that we might not know all there is to know in the area. Theologians in the past have catalogued, graded, dissected, and analyzed every possible sin in the area of sex, number and kind, gravity and punishment. If a few brave people have at

times said that sex was good, a satisfying human inclination, and that occasional or even frequent shortcomings
in the area were understandable, we have hardly dared
believe it.

One more contrast can be offered: The incident of
Jesus curing on the Sabbath. The Pharisees objected that
what Jesus did was against the Mosaic law. But Jesus
persisted, saying that curing a person was far more important than any law.

This short passage (Matthew 12:10-13) reveals Jesus' attitude about the purpose of laws. Coupled with
many other passages in the gospels, the impression remains that laws speak to something which is reasonable
and of value. They are never meaningful in themselves.
Law is observed because it promotes a common good.
Ignoring the suffering of one's neighbor out of respect for
law misses the meaning of authority.

The authority of the church has in the past been
used to multiply hundreds of laws: to leave Mass before
the priest's communion is a mortal sin; to leave after is
venial. The lenten fast is broken and sin is committed
when one eats more than twice as much in one's principal
meal than in the other two meals combined. But once the
fast is broken, there is only one sin and it is not multiplied
by eating a number of separated times. Servile work is
prohibited on Sunday, except in the interest of health or
the assistance of others.

From these contrasts, one question becomes unavoidable. How did the church arrive at that state from
what seemed to be such a different beginning? Where did
the movement away from influencing thought and behavior to demanding obedience have its origin? There was
probably no single beginning. Directions, most often, are
due to the interaction of many causes. Circumstances and
even accidents contribute to change, going backward as
well as forward.

One of the obvious currents that contributed to mis-
taking authority for unlimited power came from the

growth of a small Christian community into the religion of the empire. The conversion of Constantine brought about changes in the church which would never allow it to return to what it was. With his endorsement of the faith, Christianity flourished and achieved a respectability and acceptance which seemed a satisfying and final accomplishment. With the emperor for the Christian faith, who could be against it?

From that point in history, the message was preached to sometimes hesitant listeners with the assurance that it was the will of the emperor. The church became identified with the empire through pacts, agreements, and the mutual reassurance of benefits. It was like a holy alliance, a wedding of the secular to the sacred. But in the end, the secular was more visible.

This initial growth of Christianity under Constantine in the fourth century grew even greater in the centuries which followed. Large numbers of people joined the church. Entire countries were "converted." The results of this rapid and spontaneous development were not always beneficial. It is one thing to endorse a movement, and quite another to know something about what one is endorsing. In the case of the conversion of the empire, the net result was the presence of more uneducated Christians than the church could handle without the heavy use of authority. It seemed natural that the successors of those who were originally chosen by Jesus to preach the gospel to all nations should have divine authority to care for the church. The church was closely identified with the empire, and sometimes much of what Jesus had said was dimmed if not lost.

Jesus described the distinguishing features of the church as service, concern, and sensitivity. These traits became secondary in preference to power and command. Admittedly, no one deliberately set out to distort what Jesus said. Circumstances dictated the shape of reality. There was a pressing need for direction. The need became more acute with the passage of each century, until finally, the use of power and coercion could not be avoided. That many people in the church took advantage of the opportunity of authority is also admissible. Abusive treatment and the distortion of truth for personal advantage seem to be a part of the human fabric. Such insight is only possible in retrospect.

Although Christianity flourished, it wasn't always the best the church had to offer. If the church took consolation in the massive numbers of Christians, it also had to accept an unbelievable mixture of appalling ignorance. Most church historians agree that the faith of this time was largely superstitious. Emphasis was placed on attempting to please a demanding and distant Creator. Interwoven with this idea was the belief that the church was the visible instrument of God's presence. In that world, the authority of the church was simply accepted by Christians.

It becomes impossible to maintain such a position without assuring everyone concerned that answers to every question are available. Such certitude requires constant effort toward law and motivation. As new questions arise, there are sufficient resources in the church to adequately answer them. The image of Jesus washing the feet of the apostles has been receding.

The church was characterized during these times by what could be called "paternal" authority, which means that the members of the organization were treated more like children than adults. With such an approach, the church saw its members as incapable of making sound religious judgments, too uneducated to understand. As a good parent would do, the church took the care of its children entirely into its own hands.

During the Reformation in the sixteenth century, because of the rebellion of Luther, Calvin, Henry VIII, and others, the church called a Council at Trent. New forces were brought to bear through the definition of doctrine, and an effort was made to better organize and clarify what was being taught. But there was no relinquishing of authority, no indication that the church might do better by re-examining much of what Jesus had to say. This was not to come for a long time.

These conditions, which took centuries to develop, prevailed in the church until recent times. The authority of the church survived through the Renaissance, the age of Enlightenment, the Industrial Revolution, the age of science, and progressed essentially unchanged into modern times. If the church changed during these five or six centuries, the change had little to do with authority and, if anything, the general presumption that God's voice and will existed exclusively in the church grew even stronger.

It was an age of apparently excellent health for the institution. The church became a voice in the world, a symbol of power. Words and phrases that gave the image of power and reign became commonplace and unquestioned. We speak today of the supreme pontiff, the princes of the church, their eminences and excellencies. We describe the church in terms of majesty, governing and ruling through edicts and declarations. We speak of the papal palace, the triple crown, regal vestiture, the papal chair, the bishop's mitre. The clergy became uniformed in royal colors of purple and red, flowing robes and sashes. A hierarchy of authority descended from the highest Catholic ruler downward through cardinals, bishops, priests and clergy, to deacons and finally, to the lay people.

In reviewing the position of the church and its development of authority, there is a tendency to be carried away in the rush of righteous fervor. There is an inclination to generalize, assuming that all the hierarchy and clergy were aware of what was happening. It is unreasonable to argue that those in authority always abused their power and wanted to be hard on others. That there were many good priests and bishops is unquestionable. In those days, as always, there were and are people who reflected quite clearly Christ's exhortation to concern ourselves with the kingdom and all other things would be added.

But for all that, the church could not continue indefinitely in such a high position with immunity. Loss of credibility does not come in an instant. It begins rather imperceptibly and moves toward wider consciousness. The loss of prestige and influence came gradually to the church, through a conscious recognition that it had not always been right, regardless of its insistence and its offer of guarantees. No matter what the church had said in the past, slavery was immoral, and charging interest for money lent could not be a mortal sin. The Crusades were an embarrassment and out of focus with what Jesus had said about peace and poverty in spirit. In more modern times pressing issues were completely neglected: racism and segregation, nuclear weapons, questions about modern warfare and the possibility of obliterating the entire world, corporate responsibility, the call to minister to the poor and neglected, and the need to witness simplicity. There are those who accuse the church of so identifying itself with the state, with the powerful, the rich and persuasive, that it has lost its truer identity with the homeless and simple Jesus. Some hold that the church was never intended to have every answer, cover every situation in doctrine and morals. It is rather its mission to forgive, sympathize, show compassion, support, and to gently reassure. Still others have come to dismiss the church because of its bureaucracy. These hold there is too much internal structure: tribunals, certificates, forms, statistics, endless paperwork, commissions, organizations, and councils. Briefly, a flood of criticism has broken over a dam which had held intact for centuries.

To respond to such criticism, so often reasonable, by further entrenchment, retaliation, and recourse to the outdated reliance on authority, is to refuse to admit any fault in the church. To continue to resort to censure, silencing the voice of dissent, punishment, and vindictive retribution, is again to miss the point. To listen and to learn, without fearing the loss of prestige, to be willing to grow, even to admit past mistakes and shortsightedness, is to better exemplify the weak and erring human spirit which Jesus came to accept and even lived out in his own life.

With the Second Vatican Council we have taken a healthier direction which has to do with open and honest questions about authority and its meaning in the Christian life. In the past twenty years, many theologians have called for a thorough reexamination of much that had been taken for granted before. Did Jesus come to establish the kind of authority which has been characteristic in the church for centuries? Have we lost something of what Jesus wanted to tell us about care and service toward everyone? Are we reflecting in our lives as members of the church the same kinds of qualities of mercy and acceptance which Jesus did in his? Can these questions be answered in some frame other than authority with its need to be right?

If the present condition of authoritarianism in the church took centuries to develop, perhaps it's reasonable to expect that new and better directions will take a long time to develop also. There was a certain security connected to such an absolute church which is difficult to relinquish. The identity of many Catholics is wrapped up with the unerring correctness of the church's doctrines and morals. Some are confused and angry, see the unchangeable church as changing, and, therefore, not true and unswerving as they had been taught that it was. They are nostalgically looking over their shoulders, waiting and praying for those former times to return. They are confident that they will, and even hopeful that God might personally intervene.

There are those people who have long since left the church, judging that there is too much which is incredible. These contend that authority has been misused to avoid certain uncomfortable issues. While the church is saying one thing, it is doing another, picking and choosing its way through priorities. The church might give lip service to what Jesus said about caring for the poor, seeing to the needs of lost and alienated people, but continuing to amass funds, build cathedrals, and collect rich furnishings. They protest that a church which said so little about the mistreatment of the Jews in the Second World War, so little about the obvious dishonesty of big corporations, and the exploitation of small countries by large nations, can hardly understand the deeper meaning of authority which comes from example and living out what the church is claiming to teach.

Authority is incredible when we preach and do not do, when we are opulent by choice and espouse poverty, when we demand more from those under authority than those in authority are doing themselves. Authority is distorted when we create a need in those under authority and strictly control the fulfillment of that need.

There is a third group of people whose reaction to the history of authority and its development up to the present time is one of hope and anticipation. They hope that the church will continue to see light and make efforts to change whatever is necessary. This group maintains that the message of Jesus is still there. It has not changed. These people are convinced that the church is returning to something more meaningful, more reflective of what Jesus was saying. There is a need for continued search and willingness to grow through thinking and probing. As in any aspect of the Christian life, refusal to be enlightened is seen as the principal error. A strict holding on to the past for its own sake, without regard for what could make for a better church, is seen as a refusal of the message itself.

The documents of the Second Vatican Council speak clearly, leaving no doubt that authority in the church needs some new thinking. Words and phrases are used to signify the need to see the entire body of the church as contributing toward its healthier state. Such phrases as "corporate decisions" and "collegiality" indicate the willingness of those in authority to take a new look at the problem. Since the Vatican Council we are seeing such notable results as parish boards and parish councils on the local level. In most dioceses today there is a priests' council whose function is to assist the bishop and administrators in determining policy and drafting approaches to problems. Contrary to long-standing tradition, the bishop no longer makes decisions without consultation. Liturgy and education commissions have been created. Committees for community affairs, continuing education, local theological commissions, and dozens of other auxiliary forums have been started. These are all in the interest of effecting a more horizontal approach to authority, decentralizing the church, and giving attention to the need for equal voice.

We can add to all of these developments the progress of lay ministry, something literally unheard of before the Second Vatican Council. In most parishes, people are reading and commentating at Mass, assisting in the distribution of communion, and directing congregational singing. This can surely be seen as a corporate effort by many people to restore something of service and concern as the true ingredients of authority in the church.

One might still object by arguing that in many places there is still too little change, and what there is is incredibly slow. In many dioceses what is supposed to be renewal toward meaningful authority has become only a rubber stamp. In spite of parish councils, the pastor still makes the decisions, at least those of any consequence. Priests' councils are only on the books. The bishop still has complete control and is only paying lip service to those under him. Commissions and organizations within the system are house organs, voices which express what they are supposed to, the dependable company line.

The criticism that even the most sincere people sometimes become swallowed up by the system, is too often true. Those who work in the chancery, the marriage tribunal, or in other official capacities too easily take on an "official" attitude themselves. From that "high place" there is a temptation to see the general Christian body as the people "out there" and to regard them as lesser beings, outside the realm of what is truly important. Within the parish structure it is not uncommon to see pastors who are still holding on to the sceptre of authority, refusing any consultation, resenting interference, referring to their position and status. "This is my parish; I built this church. Don't try to tell me my job."

While admitting that these situations still exist, they are not the general rule. Much is happening in many dioceses and parishes to give encouragement and generate interest that absolute authority does not have to be the order of the day. Progress against so much history is necessarily slow, but there are beginnings which are taking place even now. Since the church has taken a new look at what is truly important, it is impossible to think that it will ever return to the state of affairs which existed before. Even admitting that some things have been slow in coming, less than satisfactory to many, we need only look at what has happened and compare the current situation to the way things were a mere twenty years ago. If the whole picture has been less than earth shattering, at least a few barriers have crumbled, some others are tottering, and there are surely more developments to come.

At the base of all this is the direction of a better theology which is asking new questions and giving answers which are reasonable, a saner response to the meaning of our purpose here. The most encouraging thread of persuasion lies in a new line of thinking about truth standing on its own merit. Where truth is evident, authority is hardly needed. If something is not true, or if it is meaningless, it will die of its own weight. Theologians are asking us to evaluate the teaching of Jesus, not because of force or fear, but rather because it is true, reasonable, and adds something positive to our lives.

To these notions we can add a further reflection. Do we merely teach truth, or do we live it out in our lives? Jesus warned his followers not to be like the scribes and Pharisees, but rather to practice what they preach. One suspects that Jesus was resorting to the use of irony here, indicating that these leaders were creating a credibility gap by too much teaching and not enough doing. The truth is important. But just as important is the person who speaks it. We are more likely to accept the authority of those who are living out what they are asking of others. A long time ago someone said, "I would rather feel compunction than know how to define it." Perhaps the principle wouldn't suffer too much if we substituted some new words and said, it's far better to see someone practicing in their own lives what they are asking us to do in ours.

A new attitude toward authority can also be seen in that there is less emphasis on fear and more on helping one another to understand. A characteristic reaction of Christians in the past has too often been one of feeling threatened. If someone made a statement which might call the church into question, too often there was reaction and warning. If a book was written with the intention of adding understanding or insight to doctrine or morals, it was too readily viewed with suspicion and skepticism. Even on the parish level, if a parishioner spoke up with a sincere and legitimate request for accountability, pastors often reacted with resolute disregard or even incivility. What have we been afraid of? Is it possible to disagree without implying rejection? Are encounters and confrontation necessarily to be avoided at all costs, responded to with insensitivity or with sanctions? Did the church really have to resort to excommunications, public denouncements, and the use of power to embarrass and mortify? Did it have to censure sincere theologians who often shed much more light into the darkness of doctrine than those who were censuring them? Was it ever really necessary to burn people at the stake for their "irresponsible" theology? Has the church ever adequately apologized?

Some theologians are now saying that leadership in the church is not necessarily or even primarily confined to those who are in "positions of authority." True authority arises from service toward others and from being a living witness to the truth that needs to be taught. We must look to those who are giving the example of such service and truth in their lives. Leaders can sometimes get distracted with the importance of their own positions and never really get around to leading. But there are truly great leaders who emerge in every age. We might not canonize them, but what they accomplish serves to enspirit the lives of the people who live with them and those who come after them. Jesus said no greater person was ever born than John the Baptist. Was that because he lived what he preached, even to death?

We are naturally attracted to true leaders and want to follow them. We readily give them the power of authority, not to tell us what to do from some high official position, but rather because long before they would ask us to do anything, they would have done it themselves, in the fullest sense, the maximum illustration. It is impossible to think of Dorothy Day or Mother Teresa, both women of enormous dedication and compassion, ever commanding anyone to do anything, certainly not something they were unwilling to do themselves. Mahatma Gandhi went without clothing and food to dramatize the awful plight of hundreds of millions of hungry people in his country. The "authority" of such a position was perfectly obvious. This is true leadership, the kind we hope for in our lives and in the church.

Martin Luther King, Jr. gave those who followed him the opportunity to cooperate with him in what he was hoping to accomplish. There is no indication that he assumed to know more in those matters than others with whom he was associated. He never repudiated or rejected anyone who wished to take part in his cause, unless that person refused to be non-violent—and even then, he turned them away with respect and regard.

There are leaders in every age, people of authority, who paradoxically avoid authoritative positions. When asked to assume offices, they do so gracefully without insisting on recognition or demanding respect for the office. There are leaders who truly lead by example and service: parents who live out the message of Jesus in simplicity and sensitivity; teenagers who resist unhealthy peer pressures and adopt values with regard for others; those who labor for social change, for peace, better opportunity and more equitable distribution of wealth, living out the Sermon on the Mount and accepting persecution for the sake of justice.

There are such leaders within the church in its hierarchy and clergy. Some bishops are beginning to invite fuller participation in decision making, not out of formality, but with a genuine conviction that there is a real benefit here. Some priests and bishops are adopting simpler lifestyles which are more in keeping with the message of Jesus. Small groups in the church, clergy and laity, are living in community, sharing their lives, praying and working together. Issues are being discussed which were never approached before: the voice of the lay person, the contribution of women in the church, the role of the priest, dependence on those outside the rectory and chancery, the need for cooperation and dialogue. These are beginnings. They are healthy and encouraging. There is no indication that they will simply run out of energy and stop. They will go on.

There are those who resist the need for renewal in the church, which naturally includes new thinking about authority and its meaning at this time. There are at least some times when each of us would like to return to what was. We would like that because it seemed to be more stable and secure. It was comforting to know that there was an answer to just about everything, what to do and what not to do.

But too many questions remained unanswered. The need for renewal is obvious, the need for a better understanding of authority as defined by Jesus. To retain a rigid acceptance of what was, refusing to acknowledge the shortcomings of authority in the past, is to settle for less than what could be. To ask for better authority is to ask ourselves to be something more of what Jesus was. To ask for better authority is to be willing to wash one another's feet, to serve in concern and compassion. It is to be willing to replace power with enlightenment, education, and understanding. It means that we understand that motivation arises through a clear perception of the meaning of the values we are trying to live. It means we are not afraid to keep asking, again and again, what it is that Jesus is asking of us and how we can carry on what he has begun.

Chapter 6

Morality

How many times have you heard someone say, "How do I know I'm doing the right thing?" How many times have you said it yourself? It's a question people have always asked. And it's a question which has never been easy to answer.

As a matter of fact, the questions about right and wrong are so important that we have made what might be called a science of them. We use terms like "moral theology," or "ethics," or simply "morality" to convey the notion that we can distinguish between right and wrong, good and evil, and we are expected to do so.

This science, if we wish to call it that, has a long history, and it hasn't always been smooth. That might be expected, because it will always be difficult for people to agree about what is good and what is bad. It often happens that one person sees something entirely differently from another. A teenager might think it's good to use marijuana because her friends do, it makes her feel fine, and it doesn't hurt her health. Her parents would probably judge that it is harmful, too risky, and leads to other

69

bad habits. For satisfactory answers to such differences of opinion, we depend upon moral judgments which take everything possible into consideration and then make a sound decision based on all that information.

You can see how the study of right and wrong can be very interesting. You can also appreciate how it has to be a very careful science, never attempting to say too much or taking for granted that morality is easy, like falling off a log.

In the Catholic church there have always been theologians who have studied morality and wanted to offer some moral principles for the good of the people. We should assume that these theologians have been sincere and honest. But because of the intricate nature of such a science, there is the possibility of erring, sometimes saying too much and at other times saying too little. The purpose of this chapter is to probe the history of morality, gently and uncritically, with a view toward gaining some understanding about good and evil. The result of such probing should help us toward living more meaningful personal lives.

To understand the history of morality, we have to go back once again to Constantine in the fourth century. This period is central to understanding the development of the church. It was from this time that Christian life and the church began to explode toward domination of the Western world. The shift of the Roman Empire toward the Christian church made possible the conversion of entire countries and tribes of people, a kind of instant religion, through an overnight transformation. While such a radical shift might at first seem wholly beneficial, it also had specific shortcomings which eventually plagued the church, even down to our own time.

Because the transition was so swift, large numbers of those converted were Christian in name only. They simply took on the label of Christianity without lasting and meaningful changes in their lives. If new convictions were integrated into the lifestyles of the common people, they became mixed up with whatever religious ideas and practices they may have previously developed. In those centuries after Constantine, religious faith was mingled in with elements of superstition, fear, confusion, and, often enough, appalling ignorance. No more could be expected. It was simply the result of what had been haphazard and ill-organized. In this context, the Western world and the church in it entered into a dark age.

The task confronting the church was mammoth. It had to deal with the entire population of Europe. Where could it begin? There was an acute need for ministry, but no effective method of training was available. What had happened so quickly created deep needs which could not immediately be met.

How could the church keep up, take up the slack, and maintain some basic order? It was natural that it would take on a strict image, resort to zealous force and sanction, issue and declare, judge and even excommunicate wherever it was necessary to maintain discipline. Gradually, most people began to look to the church for direction. The authority which church officials assumed came to be viewed as divine and irrefutable. Control was maintained by the liberal use of threats, ostracism, and even condemnation.

What about morality in this setting? In order to sustain its image and assure its members the means of salvation, the church easily assumed the office of judge and counselor in all things moral. Individual or personal judgment was discouraged; the official church could offer answers which were more certain. The notion of the unavoidable presence of sin as an integral part of life strengthened the dependency of the common people on the educated and wise judgment of the church. There was no case too remote for its pronouncement, no area in which the church could not intervene. Its position, while rigid, was the only sure way to salvation. To incur the disapproval of the church was to risk damnation.

There were some who questioned this discipline. In

the sixteenth century the protests of certain individuals, together with other "complaints," brought about the Protestant Reformation. But the church simply retrenched itself and called for stricter discipline and conscientious obedience to its laws. The Council of Trent was convened, and for eighteen years much time and energy were devoted to more clearly defining the doctrines and moral teaching of the church.

This period was one of analysis, minute dissection, and intense speculation over spiritual matters. Those involved were encouraged by their personal assurance of God's presence directing the world toward certainty. Men of approved intellectual ability took up the cause of the church, sorting and sifting doctrine and moral judgment until nothing was left for the merest question or doubt. St.Thomas Aquinas, St. Bonaventure, and St. Albert are only a few of the theologians who devoted their lives to the study of Christian morality and whose work was consulted by the council fathers at Trent. It was a period of high prominence for the church, a time of satisfactory fulfillment and power.

One might wonder how the teaching of the church could be so credible and why more people didn't call it into question. But if certainty is a basic human need, it can become the cause of submissive obedience. People were not only ready for this assurance of certitude, they were pleased that the hard work of searching out what is right and wrong had been taken out of their hands. In that sense, we all share a great deal with our forebears, we feel the same longing for what is sure and certain. Most of us are better at accepting what others say than relying on our own judgment. It seems reasonable to believe that those who have gone before us were even more susceptible to this kind of thinking.

It was through these influences that moral theology has come down to our own time. Volumes have been written on morality underscoring in detail every conceivable situation which might require moral judgment. Seminary training included extensive preparation to equip oneself for whatever situation might arise requiring knowledge about what is right or wrong. This study has been based, for the most part, on examples or cases as they were called. From an example or case of what someone might do, moral principles were learned which could be applied in similar circumstances. For example: what if a person stole fifty dollars from a poor widow? Now what if the same person stole fifty dollars from a rich merchant? Literally hundreds of individual cases were studied in an effort to gain enough principles to make sound moral judgments.

From an effort like this to cover every possible situation, it was natural that a legalistic tone came to permeate most moral thinking. Moralists tried to propose a law or laws which would govern every possible action. What eventually happened? Laws were multiplied to meet all situations, every aspect of life, and they were detailed enough to leave nothing in question. Such legalism persuaded the average Christian that he or she was incapable of judging the moral right or wrong of any act. Laws became so numerous and so detailed that it became extremely difficult to follow them.

Let us take a few examples to illustrate the point we are trying to make. All morality was catalogued in order to avoid any possible confusion. To miss one or all of the principal parts of the Mass on Sunday, the offertory, the consecration, or the priest's communion, was a mortal sin. But to sleep or read a book through the entire ceremony would be sufficient presence to fulfill one's obligation. To eat meat on Friday was always a mortal sin. But to eat soup made from meat stock was not, so long as one attempted to strain out any pieces of meat which might be there. To smoke while praying was at least a venial sin. All bad thoughts, that is to say, thoughts about sexuality and sexual expression, were always seriously sinful. To strike a priest was much more serious than to strike anyone else. To let the sanctuary lamp remain unlighted for more than twenty-four hours was always a serious sin. To send one's children to a public school when Catholic school education was available was a mortal sin. To do servile work on Sunday was a mortal sin. But to work for pleasure, as in the garden or puttering around the house, was not sinful at all. Certainly it was no sin to cook meals, wash dishes, and make beds on Sunday. To refuse the "marital" act for any other than grave reasons such as debilitating sickness or exhaustion was always serious. If one's husband insisted upon using birth control in the performance of the "conjugal act," one might submit but take care "to take no pleasure." It was a sin to laugh unnecessarily in church. It was a sin to willfully neglect one's prayers. It was a sin to attend the wedding of a non-Catholic except for a good reason such as friendship or family ties. But one could not be a witness or take an active part in the ceremony.

If this list seems long and taxes your patience, it is by no means exhaustive. As a matter of fact, it hardly touches the surface. Sin and the moral value of personal acts have occupied thousands, perhaps millions, of pages of print. Minutest distinctions have been made, measuring unconscious and hidden motivations, admitting circumstances which would aggravate or lessen culpability. The development of moral science up to the present time has been an incredible effort, a miracle of detail and analysis which defies comprehension. Theologians gave their entire lives over to secluded living, becoming voluntary prisoners in the study and judgment of every human act, with one goal in mind. How does one determine the right or wrong of it all? All this must have arisen from a sincere and direct conviction that the message of Jesus had to do with determining the exact gravity of every sin, every infraction of the sacred law.

There were many results from this development of moral theology. Perhaps primary among them was a persistent anxiety in the hearts of many people about their own acceptability. It was hard to feel secure and comfortable about one's personal life in relation to the moral law. It seemed too easy to do something wrong. And worse, one could commit sin hardly knowing it had happened. Questions were constantly arising about whether any certain criterion existed by which we could tell if we were in "the state of grace," favor with God.

A second result of this was that God was often equated with the law. Primary emphasis was placed on judgment rather than on some of the gentle qualities of parenthood which Jesus described as belonging to God's loving forgiveness. Such developments contributed to acute anxiety and a sense of helplessness in many sincere Catholics.

Still a third result came from the belief held by many people that salvation was to be attained by the observance of the law. This endeavor, coupled with the hope of coming to death without the stain of mortal sin, was the most desired response in Catholic life. Twenty years ago we spoke much more about the laws of the church than we did about simplicity of life, peacemaking efforts, forgiveness of others, and fostering good feelings in the Christian community. We looked upon observance of the law as virtuous, equal to positive acts of social justice, personal awareness of the needs of others, and our debt to them. It was possible to "save oneself" by observing the law without understanding the deeper relationship to our neighbor. We thought less of our privilege of sharing life with others, the opportunity of seeing ourselves as family, the social message of the gospel, and the need to offer the peace of Jesus to those about us. Much of this was blurred and at least secondary to the demands of the law. Much greater stress was placed upon avoiding sin at all cost and remaining in the state of grace.

Until just recently there was very little in moral thought about corporate responsibility: the notion that we are a people who work together and enjoy the possibility of salvation as a group, a community of Christians. Less was said about problems of unequal distribution of the world's goods. We might have found it embarrassing to speak of the rich exploiting the poor, multi-national corporations thriving on the exploitation of cheap labor, the acquisition of excessive profits. Because of the anguished protest of racial minorities, the church has acknowledged grave injustices toward many people. Sometimes in the past, justice, peace, conservation of the world's diminishing resources, racial inequality, painful poverty, and rampant violence were thought to be matters better left to the state.

With increased consciousness in moral development, we are beginning gradually to move in healthier directions. And the reactions of many people would indicate that we have only just begun.

At least a part of this movement has to do with laying some things aside. We sometimes ask ourselves what happened to sin. We are disappointed at the apparent irreverence of those who have no respect for the law and even reject it. Sometimes we say that the world will never be the same for all this change and movement. One thing is certain. It will be impossible to reverse the movements that have already begun. Changes in moral thinking, as revolutionary as they might seem, have been motivated by the need for a clearer understanding of what the Christian life is all about and how we can live our lives in harmony with what Jesus was asking.

We are beginning to ask openly and honestly whether the law and the scrupulous observance of it has helped us to appreciate the message of the gospel. Have we become so preoccupied with the law that we have lost the values which it was meant to uphold? To what values do laws speak? Is it enough to drive at the specified speed limit because there is a law which says so? Or is the law saying much more about respect for life, conservation of energy, and sharing the world together? Is it enough to go to church on Sunday because there is a law which says we must? Or is there a deeper value there about the need to see God as central to one's life? Is there something about worship which we might have missed? Something about receiving satisfaction from and giving strength to the members of the community who come together at church to symbolize their unity of purpose? Is there something so sacred about laws that they can never be changed? Does every law have a value which must be thoroughly understood before the law can ever be made?

Jesus came saying that he wasn't going to change the law but rather fulfill it. He spoke in terms of the great commandments, the love of God and of neighbor. He exemplified the importance of those laws by sensitivity and kindness, a readiness to serve those who were in need. He clearly indicated that one could "keep" the law and remain unjustified. He often talked about the emptiness of fulfilling the law without the necessary accompanying spirit. To go through the ritual of washing, a strict Mosaic law, to pay tithe on small items like mint and cumin and yet to neglect the larger realities, the needs of people, the offer of forgiveness, was to miss completely what it means to live out the commandments.

Jesus began his public life by announcing to the people that a new kingdom had come among them. He did not speak often in terms of law. It was only when others asked him about law that he responded in kind. He said that he was giving all of us a totally new commandment: that we should love one another as he loved us.

It is precisely here that the crux of the problem of morality can be clearly seen. Is it easier to observe every aspect of a law than to truly love one another?

We are learning to understand that our backgrounds influence how we think and act. To expect everyone to respond to moral demands in the same way is simply unrealistic. This insight marks a radical change in moral thinking in recent years. Applications of it have brought about revised notions in a number of areas. Here are some. It is unreasonable to expect the very poor to obediently observe laws which assume that everyone has an equal right to the world's goods. If one is struggling to maintain the bare essentials of life and has not received fair treatment from those in his or her daily contact, it is hardly reasonable to talk to that person in terms of justice and respect for the superfluous goods of others. Similar thoughts can be expressed in behalf of the poorly educated. More may be expected of those who have deeper understanding and knowledge. The emotionally distraught, those with extraordinary handicaps, persons whose lives have been adversely affected by poor backgrounds, and many other suffering people find it extremely difficult to observe good moral behavior.

Still other healthy changes in moral thinking are taking place in recent times. For some time now, most moral theologians have been advocating that we judge ourselves and one another by the direction of our lives rather than by the individual or isolated sins we commit. Most of us want to be morally good, seek positive directions in our lives, but find ourselves sometimes falling short of our desired goals. We tend to look upon individual sins as a cause for condemnation. Recently we have been encouraged to concentrate upon the basic goodness in our lives, our basic choice of what is decent and virtuous. In a sense, we become our own judges. We are given the privilege of examining the direction of our lives. We can ask ourselves whether we are making sound choices, intending to accomplish what is good, while learning to live with our shortcomings. It is more difficult to deceive ourselves in these areas than it is to fool others by externally keeping the law.

This attitude is a radical shift from the former notion that one mortal sin was deserving of eternal damnation. Most of us have been horrified in high school religion classes by the example of the unfortunate person who lived a virtuous life for fifty or sixty years, only to fall finally into mortal sin, be killed in an accident before going to confession, and so be lost forever.

Some people might object that this new consideration of basic choices, of judging for oneself the goodness of one's life, takes away any obligation to obey the law. And at a time in history when there seems to be so much disobedience to the law, what we need is more and stricter laws, not a more relaxed attitude. This objection is reasonable only if the Christian life has to do with merely avoiding sin in order to be saved. But if Christianity has to do with living positively, contributing to the lives of others, truly loving even the unlovable, then direction and choice in our lives are extremely more important than the observance of laws. If one observes laws without loving, there is no benefit. We can be completely lawful and still hate the laws, which, in effect, means we act out of fear. This is actually the case with many people who disobey the law when there is less chance of being caught. Think of tax evasion, bribes, swindles, padding expenses, scandalous dishonesty of every sort in government and how much more? The strictest laws govern these crimes. Yet there has possibly never been a time in history when such infractions were so numerous. Do we need more laws? Or do we need a deep change in attitude?

Let us return to some healthier changes which are taking place in the area of moral theology. We are attempting to relax traditional insistence that it is very easy to reject God. We are even going further by saying that it might be far more difficult than we had originally thought to invite God out of our lives. Certainly we couldn't do that by missing Mass on Sunday or using the name of God in vain. It is true that just as we judge the good quality of our lives over a period of time, rather than by isolated acts, so can our lives deteriorate and become basically evil through repeated immoral choices. It is certainly possible to reject God, but much more difficult to determine exactly who does it. We are appalled at the consistent presence of evil in the world. We are witness to cruel disregard of others, unspeakable injustices, callous rejection of the pleas of those who are starving, calculated decisions about death and the destruction of innocent people. The holocaust involving the Jewish people in Germany leaves us uncomprehending at the depth of evil to which we are able to descend. When we hear of political intrigue and conspiracy always involving the voluntary destruction of the "enemy," we wonder at the purpose of God's gracious creation. But in all this, two observations might be made. The usual members of the Christian community, those who ordinarily attend the Sunday liturgy, are hardly of a cruel and evil mentality. Secondly, we are only beginning to understand something of corporate guilt, the passive acceptance of evil by many of us which permits what is immoral to continue to exist. However, it is a far leap from these realities to a conscious and intended rejection of God. There may be ignorance, a lack of sensitivity toward the needs of others, too much struggle for what is meaningless and trivial, but there is less malice in most than we are sometimes prone to think.

Closely associated with this kind of thinking is a further reasoning that sin might be serious without being mortal; that is, without bringing about the death of the soul. Obviously, we are guilty at times of serious errors and even malice. But to look upon these failings as deserving of damnation is perhaps too stringent an interpretation of moral culpability.

Still another change in moral thinking has to do with questioning whether church laws can be binding under pain of serious sin. It is an interesting question, currently without definite answers but in need of discussion. Can breaking the laws of fast and abstinence in Lent be considered a serious sin? At one time, anyone other than a priest who deliberately touched the host was said to be guilty of serious sin. Women were bound not to handle sacred vessels, were gravely warned not to be present in the sanctuary without specific permission. Serious sin was attached to the obligation of keeping the altar within certain limits of shape and structure. Theologians are suggesting more leniency in these areas and asking for more liberal approaches to the sanctions normally attached to such church laws. Sin is seen more as an offense against the order of what is right, the dignity of people, our neighbors, friends, the members of our community. The church is made up of such people; and it is for their welfare that church laws are promulgated.

Much greater emphasis has been placed on God's indulgent and forgiving nature. It has been difficult for us to acknowledge the generous presence of God's unlimited goodness. It has been too easy to view God through the eyes of our individual reference, which is often distorted by our own disappointments and failures. We are tempted to see less of God and more of ourselves in our judgments and convictions. Moral theology of times past consistently engendered the fear of punishment and loss as a motive for avoiding sin. These motives are contrary to the assurance of Jesus that God is always to be seen in the light of forgiveness, ready at all times to offer reconciliation. It is true that Jesus warns about punishment and damnation, but far more often he exhorts us to rejoice in the coming of the kingdom.

Looking at what is new in moral thinking cannot be complete without some remarks about teaching and how we hope to give a new sense of choice to those for whom we are responsible. Every appeal for goodness breaks down when those making the appeal fail to embody the very qualities they are asking for in others. The serious crisis we are now facing in government arises from a lack of good qualities in many of our leaders. Too often we see graft, extortion, payoffs, bribes, deception, coverups, and issue-dodging. Moral goodness can never be expected of others when we simply tell them what is right; we must embody the same goodness in ourselves. The best way to teach others not to lie is by refraining from lying ourselves. The second best way is to admit that although we have lied at times, we have always recognized it as a moral evil. It is unbelievable that parents should drop their children off at the church door on Sunday morning and come by for them an hour later. If moral goodness is ever to manifest itself in meaningful ways, it will come from good example, practicing first whatever we ask of others.

Perhaps we need far fewer laws than we originally thought. If it is true that law has very little to do with changing the heart, it is time for new directions. It seems feasible that we could begin to throw more of our energies into values rather than laws and into seeking understanding rather than making strict demands. Sin will never disappear. We will struggle with it even to our last breath. But it is very possible that we could come to a new conviction that, even though we sin, we are capable of being morally good.

The peace Jesus came to give should not be seen as an empty promise. We should never be content to look for it at a later time, somewhere in our future. Jesus said that the kingdom is now. It is like a treasure in a field or a pearl of great price, worth every ounce of personal energy and effort. There is no greater treasure than peace. To rob ourselves of the promise by making the Christian life unbearable, a frightening experience, is to do injustice to the message which Jesus gave us. To live in peace means simply that we have grasped the inner meaning of what Jesus said about the greatest of all commandments. It is a new commandment which has replaced and fulfilled all others. "A new commandment I am giving to you, that you love one another as I have loved you."

Chapter 7

The sacraments

It's sometimes surprising what can be found in the history of the church. It's like digging into the family closet; one discovers all sorts of old ghosts there. But earnest digging can unearth some embarrassing artifacts too. Some things we'd like to forget, cover over like cracked furniture. Perhaps it's a sign of maturity that we are beginning to live more comfortably with some of our past mistakes. We are beginning to take ourselves less seriously. We admit that we haven't come along as well as we might have and that we have quite a way to go. One thing Jesus did not guarantee was perfection.

So, it's a little easier now to live without the pressures of having to have all the right answers and "facts." We are open to change. Hopefully, we will change for the better.

With these notions in mind, it's not at all unthinkable that our approach to the sacraments, all seven of them, could stand a little reshaping. There is an explanation for the way we think about the sacraments which is fairly plausible. It has to do with a kind of superstition, or at least a sense of automatically or even magically expecting too much from them. For too long now we've labored under the assumption that receiving the sacraments is enough and nothing was really expected of us personally. They were considered important in themselves, but seen as rather unrelated to our everyday lives.

It's worth remarking that we have come to this attitude fairly legitimately. We have, historically, had a consistent temptation to make too much of "spiritual" things, giving certain objects and unidentified realities a sort of mystical power. We still do that, at least some of us. Consider palm reading and tea leaves, predicting fortunes or misfortunes, tracking the stars and their effect on our lives, being careful not to break mirrors, walking under ladders and avoiding black cats. We manage to laugh at most of this, but at least inadvertently we pay homage to the unknown "power" of the objects. This is nothing new. It has been a part of human life for centuries. Did you know that the great St. Albert, teacher of St. Thomas Aquinas, wrote an entire tract on the miraculous healing effects of jewels and precious stones possessed in church treasuries? And did you know further that St. Thomas Aquinas himself, the church's greatest theologian for centuries, wrote a treatise on astrology and how the stars affect our lives? If you consider the times in which these great teachers lived, it's not surprising that they wrote some of the things they did.

It seems irreverent to compare the sacraments with reading palms and tea leaves. But strong analogies sometimes help to make strong points. The point here is that there is at least some similarity between our attitude toward the "magical" and our approach to the sacraments. The point will take some explaining and some patient pursuit; but it's there, and it becomes clearer as we understand more about the meaning of our Christian faith.

Most of us feel a need to justify what we do. We rarely say or feel what we do without explaining our actions, at least to ourselves. If, for instance, we meet someone who is a Catholic but doesn't go to church regularly, that person usually defends his or her present belief by appealing to their past. "I used to be an altar boy," or "I sang in the choir," or "I went to Catholic grade school." From there, it's an easy leap for people to say, "I'm baptized," or "I'm confirmed," or "we were married in the church," as though that defined what it means to be a Christian.

Most of us grew up in an era when religion was more formality than substance. Baptism was simply an expected ritual when we were born. Along about the fourth or fifth grade, it was expected that we would be confirmed. Parents hoped fondly, sometimes merely for the sake of looking good, that their children would "marry in the church," or if they married out of the church, would get their marriage "fixed up." We anointed up to an hour or even two after death on the basis of our belief that the soul left the body only reluctantly. We talked about indelible marks on the soul from baptism, confirmation, and holy orders, sealing us once and forever, destining us to the stage of Christian life. All the time we judged that it was the sacraments alone which were important. We got them in, had them done, and possessed them in much the same way we would open an account, pay our debts, and put everything in order. There was a broken connection between the sacramental acts and what those acts *meant* from day to day.

In recent years, however, we have begun to ask some serious questions about the sacraments. The Second Vatican Council energetically emphasized the need to question the wisdom of our former assumptions.

What are the sacraments? How do they fit into our lives? We must ask these questions because there is little evidence that the lives of many people who receive the sacraments are different from the lives of those who do not.

Again we ask, what are the sacraments? There is something about the traditional definition which has meaning. The usual description of sacraments doesn't call for radical change. It is, rather, a better understanding of the words which is needed. In our early catechism training, we defined a sacrament as "an outward sign, instituted by Christ to give grace." It is the word *sign* which deserves deeper consideration. Contrary to previous assumptions, it is not the sign which *causes* grace. The sign, rather, points something out to the community, the people around us. The sign indicates that we are trying to live out what the sacrament implies. Perhaps an example will be helpful. A sign is defined as that which leads us to a knowledge of something else. When we see two persons embracing, our assumption is that they care for each other and that perhaps they have feelings of love. If, after seeing them embrace, we learned that the couple hated each other, our reaction would be one of confusion. We would have to judge that the sign which they used had no meaning. If we visited a church while a baptism was taking place, we would assume that here were people of faith who want to pass that faith on to their child. They are willing to say to the community that they can be counted on to live out what the sign is saying. If afterward we learned that the couple involved gave no concrete evidence of Christian living and did not manifest even the slightest response to the teachings of Jesus, we would again have a reaction of confusion and have to judge that the sign they used had no meaning.

Let us consider another notion which is related to our discussion. Sometimes in the past we have used the words *ex opere operato* with regard to the sacraments. This Latin phrase meant that there was an immediate effect upon receiving any sacrament. This phrase may seem to contradict our earlier refutation of the automatic or magical effect of the sacraments. But the notion of immediate effect was always based on the assumption that the one receiving the sacrament was actually and consistently living the Christian life. This implies so much more than simply saying that one is a Christian. It means that there can be no doubt that we are Christians, because it is perfectly obvious in our daily lives. The way we act, what we say, our reaction to others, all bespeak the presence of the Christian life. This means that we tune in to what Jesus taught and Christ's presence in our lives. This presence is a fact, even though we may be periodically distracted or momentarily unaware (even at the time we receive a sacrament), but the ongoing commitment is always there. *Ex opere operato* was never meant to imply that nothing was needed on the part of the receiver.

The first conclusion that we should make, then, is that the sacraments are always saying something, not about themselves, but about the persons who receive them. They signify that something vital and real is taking place in the lives of those who receive them. Baptism should say that the one receiving the sacrament is already committed to and practicing the life which Jesus taught and encouraged us to live. In the case of infant baptism, the parents of the infant express what is already happening in their own lives. The sacrament of marriage is saying that the two persons involved have a deeply Christian love for each other. This love is the kind which Jesus advocates: tolerant, forgiving, indulgent, generous. When the couple marry, they are "sacramentalizing" that love. They are saying that the love is already there. They are in no way saying that their marriage is going to make something happen which hasn't happened already. This would be foolish indeed. It is the same with all the sacraments. They do not cause something to happen; they signify what has already happened.

What is the purpose, then, of receiving the sacraments? They are always a celebration, a rejoicing in accomplishment. It is obvious that accomplishment deserves celebration. We have banquets and award nights; we give diplomas and degrees, wear uniforms and special clothing; we reward, applaud, give Oscars, Nobel prizes, and what not else? All these rejoice over accomplishment. It is a part of our human makeup. It is our nature and our joyful inclination to be glad because of what we do. It is an infinitely wise plan which makes religion a part of that. Life cannot be compartmentalized, religion in one corner, never touching the other realities. When there is no connection between religion and life, both become boring and tasteless.

All of this brings us to another question. Are the sacraments meaningful to us as vital, dynamic signs, as occasions for celebration? Or will we have to renew our thinking, search for a new appreciation of what they were originally intended to be? Maybe the answer to the question is individual, personal to each of us. But, generally speaking, we will have to admit that for many of us the sacraments are a formality, something which we do from habit and training. How can the sacraments have meaning if one seldom attends church, gives little evidence of the Christian life, and has no interest in community or parish life? Dare we ask if the sacraments would even be valid in such cases?

Every sacrament, then, signifies two distinct realities in the person who receives them. First, that Christ is already "happening" in that person's life. And second, that this experience causes the person to celebrate. A brief examination of each of the sacraments might help us to better understand what is at work here.

Baptism symbolizes that the person baptized is celebrating his or her faith in and action around the message of Jesus. For infants, the faith and works of the parents are the point of focus. While we commonly refer to baptism as an "initiation" into the church, this should mean that there is already ample evidence that such a beginning can take place. The ceremony uses appropriate symbols to manifest this fact and resolution.

Confirmation symbolizes a logical step in embracing the fullness of the Christian life. It signifies that the receiver has come to a personal conviction that the Christian life has enough meaning to call forth a lifetime commitment. It should be a personal and studied acceptance of all that Christian living implies. The message of Jesus demands total embrace. A decision of this totality can only be the result of already hearing Jesus and resolving to live a life in accord with his teaching. Such conviction calls for celebration; we rejoice that there is satisfaction and reward in this kind of lifestyle.

As we will explain more fully in the chapter on penance, Jesus came to offer us a message of forgiveness. This implies that we are able to live as a forgiven people and that, regardless of the gravity and kind of our sins, remission is always available to us. When such a conviction is present in our lives, we are able to celebrate with peace and confidence the overwhelming generosity of God who has promised to make our scarlet sins as white as snow.

To participate in Eucharist is to signify that we have discovered the presence of Jesus in our lives. We have found him in the least of our brothers and sisters, in those to whom we have given even so little as a cup of cold water. Because of this discovery, it is a natural consequence that we see him truly living among us. The sacrament of communion celebrates our personal association with him in our daily lives. We meet Jesus in the breaking of the bread and are able to recognize him because we know him and have touched him in many ways from day to day. When the community of Christians comes together, there should already be clear evidence that Jesus is living among us. Where we are gathered together, he is there in our midst. The priest, the presider over the Eucharist, simply acts for us. He is chosen to pronounce the presence of Jesus in the bread in the name of everyone there.

The symbolism involved in the sacraments is nowhere more clearly exemplified than in marriage. Certain requirements are necessary before any couple can enter into such a union. Without love, devotion, willingness to share life, mutual consideration, and much more, there can be no true marriage, only a shallow partnership.

When these required elements are present, they naturally call for recognition and celebration.

The sacrament of orders, or priesthood, indicates the high priority of service and ministry to others. The message of Jesus is that we must continue to minister as he did. It is no small matter to teach and baptize, to care for people, to suffer for justice, to assist the poor, to be salt and light, to be last and willing to die. For a person to give his or her life fully to these is certainly a cause for celebration. This service and ministry are never reserved exclusively to ordained priests, but must be visible in the entire community. The priest meshes the gifts and service of every member into a healthy and effective interchange.

Finally, the sacrament of the sick, or anointing (what we used to call extreme unction), expresses our belief that life always has meaning, even in times of sickness and death. There is no despair nor indifference to life for the Christian. While we don't always understand individual sickness and suffering, we acknowledge in faith that God is always accomplishing good. We are trusting people, wrestling with setbacks and pain, wanting to overcome them, yet we always know that there is meaning here also. In the sacrament of anointing, we are celebrating our faith-conviction that life is never empty and meaningless, that God is always present to us. We are rejoicing that, even when we cannot understand, we can accept the rigors of existence as woven into the gift itself.

Clearly, much of what we have described can exist in a person's life without their receiving the sacraments or even knowing of their existence. Such persons could validly receive the sacraments if they chose to do so. Furthermore, every Catholic chooses to express his or her religious faith sacramentally. The purpose of this is to give those receiving the sacraments the opportunity to celebrate what is already existing within themselves. And the celebration strengthens the community by bringing together people of similar faith and conviction.

What changes, then, have taken place in recent years which will help us to better understand the sacraments? Are these changes meaningful? The answers to these questions will give us an insight which should help us get an integrated understanding and deeper appreciation of all our religious practices.

Once more, it will be better to consider each sacrament separately rather than lumping them all together.

It was standard procedure twenty years ago to schedule all the baptisms at one time, usually on Sunday afternoons after the last Mass. At a designated hour the priest went to the vestibule of the church where the baptistry was located. There he found an assortment of people, parents and godparents, family members and invited friends. Some (or even most) of these people had never seen the priest before. If he was conscientious, he would try to make the experience pleasant, encourage the people present to participate, and even offer some instruction on the meaning of the sacrament. Once it was over, there was hardly a second thought as to what had been done. It was believed by all, or most, that the ritual had been effective, independent of the intentions and dispositions of those involved. The priest was simply repeating a ceremony which had been taking place in the Catholic church for hundreds of years. It was assumed that what had been good enough for those people back there in history was certainly good enough for them.

We assumed, at least implicitly, that the sacrament was asking very little of us. With that kind of mentality, certain abuses have crept in. In too many cases, both parents and godparents lacked a sufficient understanding of the sacrament of baptism. If anything, it was considered the obligation of the church to see to the religious indoctrination of the child. Wasn't that the way it was? We might send our children to catechism later on, or even to a Catholic school. There they would learn about the church.

It was exactly in this way that baptism came to be

regarded as a ceremony complete in itself. Baptism lost its connection to the before and after. We are now beginning to recognize that the sacraments themselves are meaningless without personal involvement and active commitment. The sacrament of baptism can only be effective if parents themselves accept the responsibility of teaching their children the whole frame and scheme of the Christian life. This implies consistently teaching children to revere the gift of life, to see nature as God's personal blessing to us, to help them to pray, to teach them the love of others, to encourage them to serve their neighbors, to guide them to deep personal values of selflessness and generous love. A child could be baptized hundreds of times without effect, unless these interests were present.

The primary change we are making in our approach to baptism has to do with education, enlightening ourselves about the deeper meaning of the sacrament. In most dioceses and parishes today, baptism is given only after some preparation has taken place. This is usually in the form of classes and discussion about what faith is, how it is lived, and how we offer the community of faith to others. Particular stress is placed on the role of parents who are having their children baptized. The reason for this emphasis is obvious from what we have said about the need for personal commitment and a willingness to accept the responsibility to instruct and give example to the child.

Classes are usually scheduled over a month or six weeks with presentations on subjects which will help toward a better understanding of the sacrament. They include new looks at old subjects like original sin, the meaning of faith, the significance of belonging to a Christian community. There is an effort to invite people to a closer commitment to those things which Jesus recommended. In most parishes those leading the classes want to make them interesting, persuasive, and they want to emphasize freedom rather than obligation. The effort is toward informality and respect for what each one has to say. There

should be no force or fear. The changes are only beginning. It will be some time before they are generally accepted and appreciated. It is natural that some people
will view the changes with suspicion and attend the
classes only reluctantly in order to get the baptism over.
But the value of something new always has to be proved.
Hopefully, this will happen in time.

Some parents might decide not to have their child
baptized after they attend the preparation classes. There
might even be cases where parents would be persuaded
to postpone or cancel the baptism. Such persuasion and
decisions must be carefully weighed. Some deep thought
should be given to whether the sacrament of baptism
would have any meaning, or even be valid, if there was
no resolve on the part of the parents to follow up the
ceremony with positive and consistent effort.

Much of what we have said about baptism can also
be applied to the sacrament of confirmation. But there
are certain particulars surrounding confirmation which
also deserve discussion and renewal. In the early church,
those asking for membership were called catechumens.
A catechumen was someone who was preparing for formal
acceptance into the Christian community. Until that
time, however, instruction and certain activities having
to do with prayer, service, and good works were required
as a preparation for becoming a "full" Christian. This
preparation sometimes lasted for years, until the Christian community judged that the candidate was fully prepared and ready for acceptance. This judgment was carefully made and never off-hand. It was based on the
conviction that once the faith was accepted, it would never
be rejected, that the person involved would remain active
and fully involved in the Christian community. Even with
that much care and background, new converts occasionally did not persevere. In those days the sacraments of
baptism and confirmation were conferred together. Later
on, when infant baptism became the custom in the
church, confirmation was delayed until the person could

make a mature decision to definitively accept the faith in its entirety.

Since that time it gradually came about that confirmation was ordinarily conferred somewhere toward the end of grade school, at age eleven or twelve. There is a certain faulty logic underneath this development. It has to do with having the child confirmed before the age of independence or leaving home. This custom is contrary to the very purpose of confirmation, which celebrates the independent and personal acceptance of the faith as one's own, rather than as something that has been given by others. The result of this custom is often a lack of understanding on the part of those receiving the sacrament and mere submission to ceremony. Most adult Catholics hardly remember their confirmation. If they do, it is only vaguely and certainly with no recollection of serious commitment and transition in their lives.

A case in point. This story is told about a certain parish, which could be anywhere and of any social make-up. When it was announced that confirmation would be conferred and that those wishing to be confirmed should begin coming to classes, some sixty youngsters around the ages of twelve to fourteen showed up. The classes lasted for six weeks. After confirmation—at which the church was packed with family and friends—only four of the sixty continued to attend religion classes and many of those "committed youngsters" were literally never seen again. Each of the candidates had written a letter prior to confirmation stating why he or she wanted to be confirmed and what they intended to do after confirmation by way of service and involvement. Parents of the youngsters were asked to assure their own involvement and they readily agreed.

That something was missing and that renewal is needed becomes even more apparent in another example. Three years later confirmation was announced in an adjoining parish. This time, more requirements were laid down: applicants at least had to be in the ninth grade and were required to sign a type of "contract" before beginning classes. Preparation was to be for one year. Four absences would be taken to imply that one did not wish to be confirmed.

Some came to only one or two classes, once they had begun. After nine months about one-third had dropped out. Some who stayed had negative feelings, that they were being forced to attend the classes. Many parents objected to the program. At the meetings which parents were required to attend, only some came, mostly mothers. Once summer vacation arrived, some of the candidates were openly hostile to giving up their time. Some were conscientious and never missed a class. There was an obvious relationship between the attitude of the parents and the child. In many cases where parents did not attend church and were in no way involved in parish life, there was no improvement on their part during this time. Some of those who attended all the classes but did not go to Sunday Mass once during this time still insisted that they should be confirmed and they thought of themselves as practicing Catholics. The person offering the classes was a kind and sensitive priest, far above average in dealing gently with people. He made arrangements for make-up classes, and every effort was made to involve and interest both the youngsters and their parents.

Is confirmation an adult sacrament? Are we asking too much of younger people when we have them confirmed with no mature resolution or full knowledge of the importance of the sacrament? Can we explore new possibilities and even admit the need for fewer but far better informed Christians? Has the church become unwieldy from far too many uncommitted people?

Some theologians strongly suggest that the age for confirmation should be put off until nineteen or twenty, or even later, when a personal and mature decision can be made toward faith and practice. Even with the knowledge that many who are now being confirmed would choose not to do so at a later time, the theologians still recommend such a practice. Things of value must be earned. What comes too easily pales over time.

If more preparation and a better understanding of baptism and confirmation are sorely needed, the same need is also apparent with regard to marriage. The ever growing number of divorces in our time clearly demonstrates that the married state is suffering from poor health, and it's not getting any better. But divorces don't tell the whole story. They merely indicate that, of those who struggle to stay married, many are unhappy, drifting without real purpose, and sometimes in an agony over the pressures and tensions of married life. It is too easy to paint a depressing picture, implying that all or most marriages are problematic. This is simply not the case. All of us are aware of good, solid marriages.

But the number of good marriages is far less than the number of those in which people spend much of their energy just surviving, keeping their heads above the threat of lonely frustration.

The traditional notion in most religions has been that marriage in the church offered added help in avoiding divorce and obtaining the blessings of happiness. But there is no proof that this has been the case. As a matter of fact, since 1959 divorces have reached epidemic proportions. And in some years divorce among Catholics was more prevalent than among members of other religions. We come once again to confront the question: What meaning do the sacraments have when they are received out of mere formality?

Sadly, an overwhelming number of people are simply unprepared for the long and serious commitment that marriage requires. There is nothing of any consequence in life for which people do not prepare, except perhaps marriage. We are trained, schooled, apprenticed, examined. We are journeypersons, understudies, interns, assistants, and on probation before we are permitted to practice professions or careers. But most people simply "get married" without training or preparation, save for the conviction of love and an irresistible attraction. Because the human person is so highly subject to change, growth, and various directions, love can easily break down and diminish before the unanticipated and the misunderstood.

For too many people the wedding day marks the beginning of confusion, anger, and bewilderment over the ordinary demands of marriage. Marriage thrives on communication, mutual respect, maturity, sexuality, children, family life, and selflessness. Without these basic ingredients, marriage can be a painful and failing process.

In light of all this, the only meaning that Christian marriage can have comes from practical faith. This means that one asks to be married in the church because one believes and acknowledges in practice that the Christian message helps us to live a better life and therefore a better married life. Marriage in the church definitely does not mean that one does this because one was baptized, or was an altar boy, or because it would please one's parents, grandparents, or the whole family. As with all the other sacraments, there is nothing automatic or miraculous about marriage in church. It is, rather, a celebration of what is already happening.

And so there are some changes taking place. Couples are asked to give notice at least three or four months before their marriage. This time is used for classes, discussions, an attempt to know one's partner better, to discuss sexuality, children, the meaning of marriage as a sacrament, to talk about liturgy, and generally to prepare for the most meaningful decision and commitment of their lives. Marriage today is far different from what it was a generation ago. Couples grapple with the population explosion, women's roles, increased emphasis on material possessions as status symbols, questions about the number of children, about high mobility, and a rapidly changing and increasingly complex culture. In the face of this new world, married persons more than ever need to think out what it means to be a Christian couple.

Another change in our approach to the sacrament deals with those who have been married and are now separated or divorced. We are beginning to offer much more understanding to those who are divorced than we have in the past. We talk less of failure and bad intentions and more in terms of assistance, the need for sensitivity, and we even acknowledge that marriages sometimes cannot continue to be binding unions. There is often too much missing which should be there. We are much more concerned to help those who have met with difficult marriages. We have begun to declare certain marriages null for lack of preparation and intention. We are offering respect for one's individual conscience and not burdening those who are divorced with embarrassing restrictions and sanctions. Much of this is long overdue, and it is much more consistent with the image of a kind and generously accepting church. We must apologize to those who have suffered in the past because of resistance and even rejection. Far too many people have suffered anguish and doubt over their state before God because of the judgments of church officials who sometimes withheld sacraments, denied privileges, and even excommunicated those who happened to be less fortunate in their marriages.

Many more people today are opting not to marry. There is a freedom of spirit which has developed at this time in history, offering the opportunity of alternate lifestyles. While there is still much social pressure to be married at any cost, especially for women, there are some who refuse to succumb to the pressures of over-interested parents and other "support" groups. The experience of community, sharing one's gifts with a group of persons rather than with one, has come into sharp focus in the past twenty years. There is much experimentation in these areas, and history must wait for specific results.

Many tend to be skeptical. There is another tendency to put everyone opting for different lifestyles into one grand category, disapproving or condemning them all. We hear about people living together, being irresponsible, not wanting to make the sacrifices of marriage. Many who have chosen not to marry live productive and sometimes far more effective lives than those who do. It is impossible to generalize. It is quite possible not to marry out of evil intentions, pragmatism, irresponsibility. It is likewise possible to marry for these same reasons. It is the person who counts.

While we might not think of the sacrament of orders as undergoing any major change, there is much in this area which also deserves comment. A lot is being said about the meaning of priesthood and ministry in modern times. We are beginning to question the position of the priest or pastor as having an exclusive role in the church. If anything, the role of the priest is seen today as one which calls upon the entire people to minister to one another. Hopefully the time is past when priests were solely responsible for the entire parish, the spiritual and material welfare of it all. Happily, what the priest used to do in administration, decision-making, policy-setting, and even caretaking, is now being done by the corporate body of the parish. In most cases, the body does them better.

We talk today about the priesthood of the laity, a term which St. Peter used a long time ago. It simply means that everyone has been called into the embrace of the church and mutually shares that vocation. If priesthood has any meaning, it has to do with being asked by the Christian assembly to act in its name, to serve in its behalf. At least theoretically, anyone could be called to the formal priesthood. In the meantime, everyone shares priestly functions. This is why we have said so much since the Second Vatican Council about the role of the layperson. We are asking a great deal of one another. We are being asked to take our place, assume our role in the church, be priestly to one another. It is a healthy sign that most priests are welcoming this assistance and desire to share ministry and care with the congregation. Because we recognize that everyone in the church should have equal status, we are asking people to come forward and participate: to read and comment, to join in singing or direct the choir, to preach, to teach, to organize the parish in more efficient ways, to assist in liturgy and preparation, to be social-minded, to assist those in need, to build community. This is priesthood, holy orders at its most fundamental manifestation; and it belongs, by its very nature, to those in the parish.

Let us finally say a word or two about the sacrament of the sick. An obvious and consistent element in Jesus' ministry was his sensitivity to all who were sick. The gospels repeatedly tell us about his willingness to spend time with them, to heal them, to lay his hands on them. The people of that time brought many sick people to Jesus, those who were lame, chronically ill, even the dying. That the apostles were impressed with his sensitivity is evident from instances in their own lives. The Scriptures command us to be kind to the sick: "I was sick and you visited me." St. James directs the Christian community to care for the sick by calling in the priest, praying together, laying on hands, and anointing with oil. St. Paul suggests that the gift of healing is one that is given to many people in the community. Through all these acts, we express our own conviction that care for the sick should be a primary part of our Christian lives.

The sacrament of the anointing of the sick is the principal symbol the Christian community uses to signify its sensitive ministry to those who are ill. It is our way of saying that we are aware of the needs of the sick. We pray with them for their health, welfare, and submission to the inevitable demands of life and death itself.

In recent years we have broadened the use of the sacrament of anointing to minister not only to those who are dying, but also to those who are suffering from chronic illnesses, about to undergo serious surgery, and those who are suffering from serious illness. This seems to be a more reasonable use of the sacrament, and it takes away a lot of the fear of imminent death that was associated with being anointed.

To this attitude about sickness we should also note a new and healthier attitude toward death. We are talking more in terms of death as transition, rather than as ending. The work of Elizabeth Kubler-Ross has contributed to a better attitide toward death for all of us. The church has taken off its black vestments and put on the white garments of resurrection. There is far less emphasis on the subject of punishment. The time of death is seen more realistically now as one which calls for consolation and sympathy. Fire and brimstone have been replaced with an effort to remember the good in people's lives. No one in the church laments the passing of the somber old customs. We might miss the ponderous wheeze of the organ playing the *Dies Irae,* harking back to our grade school days, but we wouldn't want to return to that.

We will consider the sacraments of eucharist and penance separately, but in the same light as those above.

It is at least remarkable, if not overwhelming, that so much change has taken place with regard to the sacraments. But we must admit that it has only begun. The object of change is always to move toward what is better. But change of itself never guarantees that we are moving in the right direction. We have to wait for results before we can make that judgment. We might even have to take a step or two backward, or in another direction. But sincerity and honesty are usually behind our efforts to make changes for the better. Jesus said that we would know the value of persons and things by the fruits which they bear. There has been much good fruit in the renewed use of the sacraments already. It becomes a matter, then, of going forward in sincerity and faith.

Chapter 8

Eucharist

A brief examination of almost any event in our lives will reveal the rich communication involved in the use of symbols. If we attend a marriage ceremony, we are immediately struck by so much which is being "said" there, not necessarily by words alone, not even by isolated actions or gestures, but by the entire ceremony. The procession says something about "walking" into a new level of living; the coming together of the bride and groom expresses their acceptance of each other before the community; the people gathered there are saying they approve and have deep hope for the couple's happiness; rings, holding hands, exchanging vows, music, flowers, literally every aspect of the total drama gives a shade or nuance of expression which is especially appropriate to this event.

Some symbols are universally obvious and cannot be mistaken. No matter where you are in the world, it would be impossible to mistake the sentiment and intentions expressed by a couple holding hands. This is a universally recognized expression of love and its spontaneous symbol. But some symbols are highly intricate and must be learned. A blinking light on a lonely sea could mean a lighthouse, another ship, a code of some sort, or an isolated house on the mainland. But to the educated, the expression is immediate and certain. The presence of a well-dressed young woman in one's hospital room could be ambiguous until she identifies herself as representing the insurance company. But the immediate assurance communicated by the presence of another woman dressed in a white cap and uniform is unmistakable.

It can happen, and sometimes with great loss, that symbols lose their meanings or even take on new meanings which have far less significance than they originally did. Sociologists and psychologists tell us that we are always changing and losing symbols, which results in confusion and a kind of collective aimlessness when our lives could be better anchored. Take for example the family meal. It should be richly symbolic of deep and consistent expressions of familial closeness. It could symbolize the sharing and interchange of family members. It could occasion a grateful acknowledgment of the food and those who work to supply it and those who prepare it. The family meal can be a sign of hospitality toward anyone invited into the home, and a sign of the family's willingness to share with others. Other qualities which are expressed by the ideal family meal are love, concern, peaceful reconciliation through forgiveness, joy, and the acceptance of everyone present.

Very little insight is required to see that many qualities of the ideal family meal are absent in today's society. Very often there is little personal interchange, and the purpose of eating together has lost much of its original symbolism. It has become little more than a practical function for many people, much the same as other practical activities in their lives. We sometimes find ourselves eating only to satisfy hunger, or simply out of habit. In many homes, except for special occasions, eating takes place on a catch-as-catch-can basis, or even cafeteria style. The ideas of personal exchange, regard for others present, common concern and affection have been trivialized or lost altogether.

Many other symbols, which were once rich with significance, have deteriorated in meaning and substance. A marriage should symbolize an agreement between two persons to live together to benefit the entire community. Originally a covenant rooted deeply in God, marriage has come to mean something quite different for many people. Marriage today might only symbolize that a young girl has nabbed her man and been saved from spinsterhood, or that a man can now look upon the woman of his desire as his personal possession.

Sometimes we retain symbols, continuing to use them but forgetting exactly why we have them or what they were supposed to mean. Everyone still celebrates Christmas, but many "celebrants" have only a vague notion, if any at all, why they are celebrating. For many it is simply a holiday, a time for parties, eating and drinking, the exchange of presents, and all this without any conscious acknowledgment of the birth of Jesus. The holiday season has come to be an occasion for excessive commercialization and a kind of catch-all for artificial human sentiment about good will and peace on earth without any effort on the part of many people to promote and live out those human qualities.

As we begin to understand the meaning of symbols as an expression of our thoughts, convictions, and hopes, we can also get a better appreciation of some related truths. Symbols can change, be lost, or be retained without meaning. They can also have renewed effect in our lives as the result of reexamination and restatement in our culture. Some symbols have been lost or confused in the course of history. This is perhaps nowhere more apparent than in the area of religion and religious practice. Most of us cannot explain the most ordinary symbols of religion. An important example of this occurs with the meaning of the Eucharist.

When Jesus came together with his apostles for the

final meal, he gave them bread to eat with the assurance that it was his body. What significance did that have for them, for the community who followed them, and for us? How did they approach the Eucharistic meal? One thing is certain: these early Christians believed that Christ was present in their midst and that they were receiving the body of the Lord. They looked upon this "breaking of the bread" as completely different from every other meal. Even though the "Lord's Supper" was sometimes connected to regular meals, it was always viewed as the completion of the meal or as the sacred element at the end of the gathering.

But what were they symbolizing by their participation in the ceremony? Was there something there which went beyond the sacramental presence of Jesus in their midst? If we can take what St. Paul said to the Corinthians about "the breaking of the bread" as indicating the belief of the early Christians, their participation symbolized that Jesus was not only present among them but actually living within them. The early Christians wanted to say that receiving the bread was a symbol to the larger community that Jesus was still living and present among them, clearly discernible in each member of the community. In the eleventh chapter of the letter to the Corinthians, Paul says simply, "For whenever you eat this bread and drink this cup, you are proclaiming the death of the Lord until he comes." To "proclaim the death of the Lord" means that we are living out the life of Jesus which finally ended in his death. Add to this what Jesus himself said to the apostles at the final supper: "Whenever you do this, you will do it to remember me." Once again, the obvious meaning of these words has to do not only with the presence of Christ's body among us, but with his life within us. How can we remember Jesus other than by living out in our own lives what he said and did in his? To say that we remember someone without letting that person's life affect ours is meaningless.

On this basis, the early Christians regarded one another with peculiar respect and love. It was their conviction that Christ lived among them, in each individual and in the gathered community, not only at the time of the breaking of the bread, but also in their daily lives. The eucharistic meal served to strengthen and confirm this continuing presence. This meant that the life of Jesus could be plainly seen in them. By breaking the bread, they were symbolizing that Jesus was still living. It meant that the symbol corresponded to the reality.

Whenever we use the word *symbol* referring to the Eucharist, some people immediately assume that we are denying the real presence of Jesus. It turns out, however, that using that term has a new, or better, an added meaning. There is no need to deny the real presence of Jesus in the Eucharist. However, it is quite possible to receive the Eucharist without realizing its full symbolism. We do this when we receive the Eucharist without acknowledging that by this act Jesus begins to live in our lives in a unique and unparalleled way.

It is possible for Catholics to receive the Eucharist frequently without expecting any significant changes to take place in their lives. It is easy for us to think that we should receive the Eucharist regularly simply because it has been recommended as a pious practice. But the deeper significance of our participation in this sacrament should be that we are daily living the life of Jesus, and this should be perfectly evident in our lives. In this sense, with the early Christians, we are "remembering" Jesus in the breaking of the bread. We are living "the death of the Lord until he comes."

Just as much of the symbolism surrounding our family meals has been lost or confused, we must admit that something similar has happened with the Eucharist. We still revere the sacrament, adore Jesus in the real presence, and have a body of laws surrounding our use of this sacred reality. But we are less conscious of the reality the sacrament symbolizes. It's easy for us to talk about visits to the Blessed Sacrament and forty-hours devotions or to lament the passing of ceremonies like benediction and all-night adoration. But it's important to see the Eucharist as involving our personal participation in living as Jesus did.

When I was a student in Rome many years ago, we looked forward each year to an annual trip to Orvieto for the celebration of Corpus Christi, the Body of Christ. It was a festive display of our faith in the real presence of Jesus in the Blessed Sacrament. Thousands of people took part in a long procession around the city, singing and praying, hoping to show the depth of their belief, their conviction that Jesus had come into the world and even now was among them. There were always many bishops and at least a cardinal or two who added to the splendor of the occasion. The Blessed Sacrament was held aloft by the highest church dignitary there, carried in procession for all to see and adore. Splendid vestments, reserved for just such an occasion, were used. The celebrant was dressed in the richest robes, cape, and humeral veil, brocaded and embroidered silk. The monstrance containing the host was of polished gold, richly encrusted with costly jewels. The silk canopy was held high above the head of the celebrant, who slowly processed through the city as the choir sang majestic hymns. *Pange lingua gloriosi*— O glorious food, the mystery of the body of Christ; *Ecce panis angelorum*—behold the bread of angels; *O sacrum convivium*—Oh sacred and lifegiving bread; *Tantum ergo sacramentum*—We have come to adore the sacred sacrament.

We returned to Rome in the evening, uplifted by our experience, strengthened in faith, and renewed in spirit. It was a hallowed tradition which manifested our belief that the presence of Jesus among us was a reality to be cherished above every other. It was an emotional experience which left us high for days, charged with the belief that our Catholic faith had great significance and was a true rock of security.

But it was also true that too much in our lives remained unchanged. When we received communion the next morning at Mass, we failed to make the connection with the life of Jesus in us. It was too easy to forget that the procession at Orvieto wound around huts and shanties where many people lived in abject poverty. In the rush of religious fervor, it was too easy to ignore the misery of poor health and undernourishment in the faces of many of the people. We mistook the anger of some we passed in procession as a lack of understanding, when it was actually a reproach for our lack of sensitivity to the real needs of those who were tired of life as they experienced it and were waiting for the "Body of Christ" to console and comfort them. We identified our faith with the triumph of that occasion, naively assuming that God had to approve of all we were doing. We felt that the richness of the scene, bishops and cardinals arriving in black limousines, hundreds of well-dressed clerics, served to honor Jesus, inspire the people, and show forth a strong faith. Admittedly, our thinking lacked the depth to see that all that took place there deserved deeper consideration, a raising of awareness.

There is really nothing wrong with processions honoring the Blessed Sacrament. Devotions which fostered an awareness of Jesus in his sacramental presence have served meaningful purposes in our lives. Benediction, forty hours, visits to the tabernacle, and adoration have helped many people to appreciate the gift of the Eucharist, the breaking of the bread. But is it possible that we use these and other religious practices only as formalities, avoiding the deeper issues of true conversion and acceptance of the full life of Jesus? Jesus came into the world to bring the good news of consolation, ministry to the poor, a generous sharing with those who have little by those who have much, a righting of wrongs, and a demand for justice. So we are here now, with the life of Jesus in us, and a mandate to carry out that good news in our time. To spend our time in devotion to Jesus, however, praying to him, receiving him, without letting any of that mandate touch us personally, is to miss the point of his enduring presence in the world. Jesus came to cast fire on the earth, to show us how to live his life in the world without being suffocated by accidentals. It is possible to have a devotion to the Blessed Sacrament, even to receive communion regularly without being touched by the real life of Jesus.

St. Paul told the Corinthians that they shouldn't receive the bread or the cup unworthily. This has more to do with belief and living out that belief than it does with being free from sin. As a matter of fact, sin arises when we neglect the service which we owe to others, when we isolate ourselves as if the needs of others did not exist.

Little wonder then that we are witnessing dramatic changes concerning the Eucharist in today's church. This does not come from irreverence or lack of appreciation of the tremendous reality of the sacrament. If anything, it arises from just the opposite, a deeper understanding of the reality involved. "Unless you eat my flesh and drink my blood, you cannot have *life* in you." What is the life of Jesus? How do we have his life in us? It was the life of Jesus which moved Peter to say: "He went about doing good." Paul was speaking about the life of Jesus when he said: "He emptied himself, becoming obedient even to dying." And John: "He came unto his own and his own received him not. But to as many as did receive him, he gave the power to become the children of God." It can only be by reason of our belief that the life of Jesus is possible in us that we can realistically approach communion, the receiving of Jesus. It is about this concept that theologians have had more to say in the past few years.

Much has been said recently about the Eucharist demanding our response, about our doing what the Eucharist implies. The talk about bringing the sacramental Jesus into our daily lives by diminishing what had become too mysterious about the simple reality of the presence of Jesus has become confusing to many people. It almost seemed like we were taking something away from our belief in the Eucharist. In order to lessen our sense of distance from the sacrament, we have begun to use terms which are better suited to our times. The word *transubstantiation* has become less effective in speaking about the Eucharist. Theologians are defining less, admitting the impenetrable mystery, but trying harder to describe what the Eucharist means and how it fits into our lives. They are emphasizing how the Eucharist relates to sharing the life of Jesus as a community of believers, celebrating his visible presence among us. They are focusing upon the setting of a family meal where food is taken and eaten as a sign of our willingness to share our food with others. Theologians go so far as to say that if we haven't found Christ among the people in our daily lives, and if we aren't serving him in trying to fulfill the needs of those around us, we are bringing a certain dishonesty to the sacrament. They even go so far as to say that *true* reverence for the Eucharist could not be shown in ornate tabernacles, rich vestments, careful handling of the "sacred species," and a complex structure of rules and rituals. All of these can only have meaning when the greater reverence of bringing Jesus into the world, into the lives of those around us, becomes perfectly evident in our own lives.

There is a tendency in all of us to accept things as they are and to look upon change with suspicion and mistrust. What was good enough in the past should be all right for the present and the future. But in certain cases we have found what was thought to be good enough for the past turned out to be positively harmful to the message which Jesus gave us.

The process of renewal has begun, and much of our thinking about the Eucharist has to be reframed in light of new knowledge about the sacrament. We have begun by asking how we can best emphasize the connection between Eucharist, the body of Jesus, and our daily lives.

The answer to that question begins with seeing the celebration of Eucharist as not removed from, but at the very heart of daily living. We have a tendency to isolate the sacrament, as though church attendance and receiving the sacraments were something above life itself. Perhaps we find it easy to reserve all our religious activity for Sunday, a once-a-week affair with little daily carryover. This may seem exaggerated to some people, but it is generally a fairly accurate appraisal of Catholic life.

So we begin by trying to bring the Eucharist "into our daily lives." We want to show that there is no separation between the Body of Christ in the church building and the Body of Christ in our homes, on the streets, at our work, and in our daily activity. We began by bringing the altar closer to the people in church, giving the impression that the priest and the people are about the same thing, celebrating the presence of Jesus in our lives. We use our own language so that all can see and hear what we are doing. We minimize repetitious prayers and elaborate ceremonies; we try to speak clearly; and we are trying to see the full reality of the Eucharist.

We have begun to think of communion in the setting of a meal with all of its meaningful symbolism. We talk about the Christian "family," the gathered people, being called together to share this gift, the presence of Jesus, in the breaking of the bread. We have tried to see the ceremony of Eucharist as similar to family gatherings: speaking to one another, listening as others speak and read, singing together joyfully, eating, sharing food around the table as a symbol of our efforts to give nourishment to those who need it. We are aware that true ceremony cannot be cold and informal. We have to get away from quick and sometimes haphazard rituals which are based on the false notion that they are automatic and need no personal input. The ceremony surrounding the Eucharist must be friendly, gathering us together as a people convinced that we are related to one another in the faith and in life. It should be unhurried, comfortable and relaxed; it should have the warmth and ease we feel at supper with a friend.

In order to bring about meaningful change, we must examine what has become lax and dry with a view to making it more alive and vibrant. Small hosts that hardly look like bread can scarcely have any meaningful symbolism. Bread baked by members of the community and brought from their homes has much more meaning. Bread is a common food for all people. Small, antiseptic-looking white discs do not even look like food, and they tend to make the sacrament a mere formality. Jesus certainly used real bread at the Last Supper, passed it to his apostles, who chewed it and relished its taste. The use of the little hosts is a far more radical departure from tradition than the restoration of normal bread as an acceptable material for the Eucharist.

Eating, historically, has always involved handling food, from hand to mouth, tasting and chewing. It is certain that this was the procedure used at the final supper. To insist that communion is so sacred that we must depart from this and devise a whole new method of taking the Eucharist in order to show reverence, is to miss its meaning completely. Is it possible that we have treated the Eucharist with such pious delicacy that we have missed its true implications, its demand for flesh-and-blood response in service and respect for one another? Does closing one's eyes, extending one's tongue, letting the host dissolve before swallowing, seeking an intimate and exclusive union with Jesus have relevance to people around us, the daily grist of life's demands? Admittedly, it could; but to receive bread as food, passed from hand to hand, eating it by chewing and swallowing, and remembering Jesus in the breaking of this specially prepared and consecrated food seems to say more about its connection with our lives.

What about the cup? The words of the Scripture are clear. "After the supper was over, he passed the cup among them saying: Take and drink, this is the cup of my blood." Isn't it more in keeping with the original ritual to pass the cup at the time of the Eucharistic celebration? When did we begin reserving that to the priest and why? The danger of spilling? Wasn't that danger present at the supper? The danger of infection? Is it higher here than passing the hors d'oeuvres at a party? The addition of the cup to the reception of communion underscores and completes the symbolism of the total life of Jesus, flesh and blood, blood which he poured out for the good of people. It gives meaning to his exhortation to all of us to go and do likewise.

We sometimes assume that renewal in the church has taken place only in the past few years, that the church was stable and unchanged for all the centuries of its existence up to our time. We are forgetting that many changes have taken place over the course of history and that reform and growth are a sign of health and progress. Consider how fifty or sixty years ago our attitude toward receiving of Eucharist was shrouded in a mysterious awe and fear. At that time and up until just recently most people very rarely received communion. Somehow they had come to believe that they were unworthy to participate, that they were too sinful. This was a total misconception, springing from the notion that the Eucharist was for those who were perfect, sinless, rather than a source of healing and forgiveness. It was only at a later time, through a continued effort on the part of the church, that a more relaxed attitude was formed. Through education and gentle persuasion, especially through the teaching of Pius X, the age for receiving communion was lowered. The deemphasis of laws is now understood to be an important step in Catholic growth. Frequent communion is encouraged, and participation at Mass without communion is viewed as something less than complete.

One sometimes hears criticisms of change and renewal in the church as if it was all a conspiracy by people who were seeking change for its own sake. It is easy to imagine that there are people who are deliberately bent

on bringing the church to ruin. But a cursory study of
the documents of Vatican II will reveal the source of much
of what is happening in the church today. Theology expresses what we can know of God and how that knowledge
will help us to understand the purpose of our lives. We
must always avoid formality, empty ritual, and meaningless lip service which threaten genuine religious truth
and the practical living-out of our faith.

No one is maliciously trying to subvert the church.
There is no evil intent in those who are trying to present
the Eucharist, or any other aspect of the church, as appealing, credible, and in touch with the lives of those who
believe. Theologians and liturgists are making an honest
effort to see religion as related to daily living. Growth
and change always require energy, response, and active
participation in whatever changes are indicated. For the
first time in centuries we are being asked, even begged,
to take our part, make our contribution, see ourselves as
personally called to a new stage of religious response. We
cannot do that without energetic study, discussion, and
participation. Renewal means that we must relinquish
some old securities in our backgrounds. Religion can
never be automatic, done for us by someone else, the
priest for instance. It was not meant to be a galvanized
security against the world's problems. Religion does not
guarantee, nor did Jesus guarantee, comfort, ease, and
peace. It rather demands a willingness to accept the normal tensions, the stress and problems of life. God has
given us the ability to build the earth. The Eucharist is
the presence of Jesus in the world and our reception of
Jesus into our midst. It symbolizes to all who will see and
hear that we are up to the task.

Chapter 9

Penance

When we talk about confession, the sacrament of penance, the subject calls up memories in us almost without limit. We can easily conjure up visions of standing in line in some quiet church on a Saturday afternoon or evening, knowing that we were about to engage in a holy act, yet not quite sure of the meaning of it all. We were always at least vaguely uncomfortable, sometimes intensely so, depending on the sins we were about to confess. We didn't question the necessity of going there; we saw it as part and parcel of our religious belief, and we only wanted to get through with it as quickly as possible so as to rest easy for another month or so.

There were also some incidentals which added to or detracted from the experience: our hope that the priest wouldn't recognize our voice, especially if we had something "big" to say; that we could go to the priest of our preference, who gave lighter penances, was less inclined to sermonizing, or was even a little hard of hearing; and whoever he was, that he wouldn't keep us too long, so we could avoid the suspicious glances of other people when we came out.

Sometimes, and with some folks more than others, it was impossible to get that sure feeling that all was forgiven. So we went back again. Some spent hours in agony over their imagined failings. They depended on the patience of understanding priests who wanted to help them, assured them of forgiveness, but all too often unwittingly pushed them more deeply into scrupulosity.

At best, we approached and still are approaching confession with mixed feelings. Sin is never an easy reality to face. It is the last discovery we want to make about ourselves and certainly the last revelation we want to make to others.

But try as we will, sin is a part of life. It is a reality we have to deal with from the age of reason until our old age. St. Paul said that sin is a constant and never ending struggle. What we want to do, we have great difficulty doing. What we would like to avoid becomes a constant source of consternation. Jesus indicated the pervasive nature of sin by declaring that even just people fall seven times a day. If Jesus and Paul aren't convincing enough, we only have to look honestly at ourselves. There are times when we are truly grateful that only we know our sins. At least occasionally we are all surprised at our capacity for evil. Just when we think we have arrived at a higher level of virtue, something sets us back, makes us reconsider, and reminds us that we are human.

Jesus came to assure us that beyond every other quality in God, there is an unbelievably generous forgiveness of sin. This summary is completely accurate. It is Jesus' principal message and it relates to everything he says and does. Jesus comes to tell us that no matter how great our sins, God forgives them. This overwhelming news is so graphically represented in the life of Jesus that it cannot be missed. It causes anger and jealousy among the officials of the Jewish religion. It upsets longstanding tradition which demands that sinners be shunned and punished.

Jesus continues to reenforce this message not only by talking about God's forgiving love for sinful people, but by the example of his own response to sinners. When the crowd is ready to stone a woman to death because she was caught in the act of adultery, Jesus neutralizes the whole scene by reminding the leaders that everyone sins. After everyone leaves in discomfort, Jesus kindly forgives the woman. It is remarkable that he doesn't take the opportunity to give her a little sermon on the wages of sin, he simply tells her to avoid that sin in the future.

The message of God's forgiveness is further emphasized by the kind of company Jesus prefers. Our natural assumption might be that Jesus, the Son of God, the Messiah, would begin his mission by seeking the approval of and associating with the important persons of his day. He might have done well to become a Pharisee, study the law, be appointed, and then change the system from within. But the contrary is true. Jesus began his public life by associating with very common people, what we might call the lower class—fishermen, tax collectors, manual laborers. If that wasn't enough, he made friends with prostitutes and extortionists.

Finally, Jesus emphasizes that he is giving us an example. He assures us that he is asking us to do exactly what he has done. He declares that we cannot expect to be forgiven except in the measure that we forgive. When Peter questions the need to forgive and asks how many times, Jesus says that as often as people offend us we ought to be willing to forgive them. To expect forgiveness without forgiving is ridiculous. It is like like the steward who begged to be relieved of a large debt he owed his master and then wouldn't forgive his fellow servant a very small one.

After the resurrection, when Jesus appeared to the apostles for the first time, he began with a greeting of peace and then immediately raised the subject of forgiveness. He reminded the apostles that they had the power to forgive sins, and that this power was such that if they decided not to forgive, there was no way that forgiveness could take place. Here is an instance of God's acting through us: if we do not forgive one another, not even God can break through this barrier in our hearts.

It is difficult to trace the history of penance from the beginning of the church. One thing is certain, the present structure of confession developed very gradually. Many generally accepted practices in the early church lasted only for a time and then fell into disuse.

In the very beginning there doesn't seem to have been any form of confession or reconciliation. Early Christians hoped to avoid sin until they would die or Jesus would return. Many sincere people put off being baptized until they were at death's door. They believed that baptism remitted all sin and that it was worth the chance of postponing the sacrament in view of the possible loss of grace.

When forms of confession did begin to appear, they were much different from those we know today. Some historians hold that there was a period in the church when confession could be made only once in a person's lifetime, and for a time it was believed that certain sins could never be forgiven. When confession was made, public penances were imposed, and some of them lasted for years. It also appears that penances had to be completed in full before a person could be restored to membership in the church. These were difficult times and there seems to have been a very rigid approach to the granting of God's forgiveness. An additional inconvenience arose from the fact that for some time only bishops could judge sins and offer absolution.

But gradually the situation began to improve. By the seventh and eighth centuries, instances of confession as we know it began to appear. In some places in Ireland and in parts of Europe, monks and priests began to hear confessions. Frequent or at least repeated confessions were made. From that point on, the complexion of penance began to change quite dramatically.

It is reasonable to ask why the practice of confession evolved the way it did. While there may be no satisfactory answer to this question, we can say that there was a certain human logic involved. If people feel a basic need to be forgiven, some visible way of dealing with their sins, it seems natural that they would seek better forms than those which existed in the early church. People then, as now, felt the pressing need of forgiveness. This is especially true after what Jesus taught and said.

Confession was not a practice in the early centuries of the church. It is certain that St. Peter never went to confession as we know it, nor St. Paul, nor any of the apostles. To picture the members of the early Christian community lining up for confession to prepare for the Eucharist is simply false. Again, someone might imagine the crusaders seeking absolution before setting out to conquer the holy land. But not so. We can assume that people who were devout and trying their best, but still having to deal with sin, simply had to trust that God was somehow forgiving. We can also assume that people formed within themselves a kind of theology which allowed for the possibility that God forgave them. But this trust remained in the hearts of good and sincere people, and it did not find its way into the official teaching or practice of the church. We can assume that people in the early church believed that God was more forgiving than the official church taught. We might think that theologians, popes, and bishops make up theology and are solely responsible for its development. But true theology is an expression of what the people believe. In the case of confession, people simply could not deny the evidence in Scripture, the life of Jesus, that God is forgiving, that he accepts us even after we sin and readily restores us to full family membership.

Gradually, the church began to accept the sacrament of penance. Regular recourse to confession became a standard part of religious practice. The word *confession* has come to be synonymous with the word *Catholic* in recent times. Its particular significance is known to just about everyone.

Confession hasn't been without its troubles, however. Even though the practice has brought comfort and consolation to many, it has also caused confusion and anguish. We have surrounded confession with a certain legalism, a businesslike dispatch which smacks more of a courtroom procedure than the generous mercy of unconditioned forgiveness. Confession has been a stumbling block for many Catholics. Some have left the church because the patient forgiveness of Jesus has been poorly represented in confession. Many others have simply assumed there must be other means of forgiveness, and they wonder whether God ever intended such discomfort and embarrassment over the sins of good people.

Somehow, and perhaps it was from the beginning, a certain technical approach crept into the use of the sacrament. We saw confessing our sins in a general way as insufficient. It was not enough to say we had sinned. The demand was rather for detail, a concern with numbers, circumstances, what kind of intention, grave sins as opposed to those considered less serious. A legal atmosphere surrounded the practice. Such care for detail, fear of getting it wrong, hardly leads to comfort and peace. And yet confession should do just that.

The practice of confession has also suffered from overdevelopment. Repeated confessions have been encouraged as a source of merit. Confession was encouraged even when only small sins were told, even when no sins were committed and only past sins were mentioned. Daily confession was regarded as an approved pious practice, and it is said that many holy people practiced it devoutly. This sort of practice should not be condemned outright. But perhaps we should trust God's forgiveness to a much greater degree. Is forgiveness that difficult to obtain? While some people might have used frequent confession with balance, there were many more who used it as a temporary and unrealistic relief from deeper psychic disorders.

Because so much emphasis has been placed on confession, we have come to disregard other meaningful forms of forgiveness. We speak less of prayer, fasting, alsmgiving, and the Eucharist as means for the remission of sin. The history of confession shows a preoccupation with the telling of sins and less emphasis on the effectiveness of these other actions. The church has stressed confession to such a degree that we have neglected other forms of forgiveness.

Is it possible that serious sin could be absolved in some way other than confession? Can forgiveness of grave sin be achieved in any other way? The answers to these questions are complex. But theologians are beginning to offer some new thoughts. The cause of this new thinking centers around a better understanding of the individual, his or her sincerity and honest disposition to do what is good. Moral theologians are beginning to talk more about basic attitudes. They are saying that *mortal* sin is not so easily definable. What is mortal sin? Is it a total rejection of God, a denial of faith and God's purpose in creating us? If this is the case, it is difficult to imagine that the ordinary, sincere Christian very often commits mortal sin. It is true that there might be instances of sin, sometimes even serious in nature, but hardly a complete rejection of one's fundamental relationship with God. When such an absolute rejection does occur, there is a definite need for confession, a visible sign of one's desire to restore the former relationship.

It is interesting to note that Jesus never heard confessions, at least as far as we know. There were dramatic instances of forgiveness, as in the case of the prostitute who washed his feet, but no record of a detailed accounting of sins. Jesus said, "Because she has loved much, much has been forgiven her." Does this mean that love is by far the most important disposition necessary for the forgiveness of sin? In the past we have said that Jesus already knew the sins of the persons he forgave, so there was no need of confession. This answer seems somehow out of touch with the question and misses the point.

From the gentle attitude which Jesus repeatedly showed toward sinners, developments have taken place in the church which have obscured the exercise of Christian forgiveness. Recently many Catholics have begun to reevaluate the meaning of confession in its present form. Legitimate questions may be asked about how the sacrament is received. Is it necessary to emphasize the element of mystery as much as we have? Can there be more comfortable approaches to confessing one's sins?

For some people, the dark secluded confessional has been a hindrance. It is true that confession can never be completely without stress, but many feel significant improvements could be made. The darkness and anonymous whispering are often threatening; they engender a distinct uneasiness in many people.

Against this background we can now begin to discuss how such a questionable experience might be improved. We should begin by emphasizing again that the history of confession is one of gradual development. At no time in its history was it locked into a permanent form, incapable of improvement. Change is and always has been possible.

It will be of the utmost importance as we try to improve our approach to confession to remember and appreciate what Jesus said and did about the forgiveness of sin. It is as though many of us have forgotten or disregarded the compassion and understanding which were so much a part of his approach to the sinner. The example of his total mercy toward those in need should once more become the base of our approach to one another. To discuss confession only with regard to detail, structure, and legal fulfillment is to approach forgiveness in a way which Jesus did not intend. We must continually ask ourselves whether what we are doing is how Jesus would have done it. Can we imagine him sitting in a confessional, hearing endless lists of mostly petty sins, giving penances of Our Fathers and Hail Marys, sometimes using strong admonitions toward young boys because of their bad thoughts, criticizing an honest and sincere young married person for using birth control, warning those who missed Mass on Sunday? How would Jesus assist the sinner? That single question is the most important one in our consideration.

Hopefully, this one issue is at the heart of the changes which have recently occurred concerning the sacrament of penance. The question has to do with making the experience more meaningful, a better reflection of what God intended through Jesus.

The revision begins with something as simple as changing the name. If the word *confession* has a fearful connotation for some, it is far better to use words like *penance* or *reconciliation*. This might not help those who are older and accustomed to earlier terminology, but it encourages a better attitude in those who are coming along. These words, especially *reconciliation,* contain the notion of conversion, change of heart, and they get away from the emphasis on telling our sins as a condition for forgiveness.

Let's return for a moment to how Jesus dealt with sinners. Some points should be clearly noted. Reconciliation was always an open affair with Jesus, an eye-to-eye encounter. There were always specific elements present: the expression of forgiveness, understanding, and at times, a remark or two. More than these, there was an attitude of kindness. Can we do less in offering forgiveness to one another? The introduction of face-to-face confession seems an unprecedented departure from the tradition of the confessional. But it is only a return to what is more normal, more in keeping with what is human in us, a better re-presentation of the personal approach of Jesus. If the word *tradition* means handing down what is meaningful from one generation to another, then face-to-face reconciliation is truly traditional.

Because of this rethinking, most parishes have set up a room which is designed to offer the option of speaking directly to the priest, face to face. This presents the opportunity to pray together, to read a short passage of Scripture, to converse in a friendly way, and perhaps to offer advice in a pleasant atmosphere. The emphasis is on equality between the persons involved. There is no darkness, no whispering, and the situation is more readily perceived as genuine in the world of real people and normal circumstances.

Because change, especially in the church, is always difficult for some people, there has been an effort to be sensitive to those who find it impossible to make this new transition. Private penance, the use of a screen to preserve anonymity, is still an option. No one should be forced or compelled to face-to-face reconciliation.

Another form of penance which is being encouraged in parishes today is "communal penance." This new mode comes from our recognition that a parish should be a Christian community, a group of people who do things together. This means that a community wants to put the message of Christ into practice in much the same way the early Christians did. They came together to pray and worship, to look after one another's needs, and feel the presence of the Spirit of Jesus in their midst. This idea of Christian community might seem somewhat theoretical right now, but it is a goal toward which we can strive. It is also a reality which is much needed in our fragmented lives.

A Christian community should always be in the process of reconciliation. There should be no permanent separations, no rancor or rejection. We should draw enough strength from one another to move into the larger community with attitudes of acceptance and forgiveness. Communal penance is a symbol which can express our willingness to forgive and our constant need to be forgiven by others. It acknowledges that all of us sin and all of us need one another. It further says that when we sin, we are offending the very members of our community, our family, wives and husbands, brothers and sisters, and

friends. It is in this setting, in the community, that forgiveness should be sought and obtained.

Communal penance is an opportunity for the members of the parish, the Christian community, to come together, admitting the presence of sin in the members,
and confidently accepting forgiveness. This form of penance can take place periodically and there is a certain
ceremony involved. Songs are sung, Scripture is read, a
homily may be given, and a general examination of conscience is offered. The chance for private reconciliation is
offered for those who wish it.

Another aspect of renewal with regard to the sacrament of penance has to do with seeing joy in the forgiveness of sins. Jesus said, "Repent, for the kingdom of
God is here." Repentance brings about the joy of achieving
a desirable goal. We have too long looked on the sacrament of penance with doubtful comfort. We think of God's
regard for us as tentative at best, a holding back if everything is not exactly right. The old approach to penance
left room for doubt, a continuing anxiety that maybe we
hadn't done it all and still had some debts to pay. There
might have been less cause for celebration, no confident
assurance that our sins were truly forgiven.

Jesus often speaks of the peace he came to give us.
He repeatedly assures us that we do not need to be afraid.
He has told us not to fear because he has overcome fear.
Even the Old Testament, as harsh as it sometimes seems,
gives the assurance that if we are a faithful people, God
will accept us and be our parent. Even if our sins be as
scarlet, God could, by his generous forgiveness, make
them white as snow.

If this is true, and it is certainly at the heart of our
Christian faith, then there is great cause for rejoicing.
The forgiveness of Jesus is unconditional. The only disposition we need is faith enough to see ourselves in need
of remission and restoration. There is nothing in the message of Jesus that insists we confess it all perfectly, pay

attention to legal requirements, or concern ourselves more with getting it right than with faithfully accepting forgiveness. The sacrament of penance, then, should surely be more celebrative than it has been in the past.

The subject of penance and reconciliation has caused considerable concern lately. Many lament the fact that frequent use of the sacrament is waning. Some ask what happened and why people are not going to penance as regularly as they did in the past. Is this a sign that our faith is weaker, that the church and the message of Jesus are losing their appeal? Periods of transition are always periods of disturbance. It is good to relax and wait for things to settle into a new pattern. The changes concerning confession and the theology of forgiveness have certainly not ended. Then, too, it may be that we are learning that frequent penance may not be as important as we had thought. We are certainly thinking more about other means of forgiveness, as we mentioned above. We must begin to emphasize even more prayer, charity to others, fasting, and the sign of forgiveness in the Eucharist. The sacrament of penance lends itself to a community setting, people celebrating forgiveness together.

The sacrament should not be relegated to some corner of the church where it has little effect in our lives. We are always in need of forgiveness. The sacrament of penance is a visible and convincing sign that we are a forgiven people. It speaks to the progress we have made in the area of sin and forgiveness from the early days in the church. It symbolizes our faith that God is a forgiving God of tenderness and compassion. We should always be using those symbols in one form or another. The sacrament of penance offers an intimate contact with the God of mercy and comfort, something we all need in our time. It is an essential way of expressing our belief in the message of Jesus.

In *Trinity,* the celebrated novel by Leon Uris, there is an all too familiar account of the "confession" of Finola Larkin to Father Lynch. It revolves around the old and familiar theme of sex. Finola, a married woman with a number of children, is driven by guilt to confess that for years she has withheld "serious" sins. In spite of her fear, Mrs. Larkin says to the priest, "I have been the wife of Thomas Larkin almost twenty years and I have sinned all during the marriage . . . I have always enjoyed the pleasures of the flesh . . . I've almost always enjoyed the sexual act." The priest's immediate response might have been typical for 1850 Ireland: "That's quite unnatural you know." If it wasn't already, the whole encounter became a nightmare from that point on. Father Lynch insists on details and descriptions, and he cautions that nothing be left out. He concludes that the relationship between Finola and Thomas Larkin has been the work of the devil. He is not at all sure that he can offer forgiveness, and he finally consents on the condition that Finola never have sexual contact with her husband again. He further insists that her youngest son must become a priest. One gets the impression that Father Lynch is much more offended than God could ever be. The result of this "forgiving" encounter brings about the eventual alcoholism of Thomas Larkin and the complete breakdown of the marriage. There is no imaginable similarity between this encounter and the compassion and understanding of Jesus.

Perhaps the example is unfair, exaggerated to make a point. But it is too true that many people have suffered unnecessary pain from lack of understanding and the abuse of the sacrament of penance. The renewal of this sacrament would be necessary even if we had been much more sensitive. We can certainly hope that experiences like those of Mrs. Larkin would never happen again. But more, we can hope that penance will be seen as a source of hope, the assurance of God's forgiveness, and the final conquering of useless guilt which has been far too prevalent in our Catholic lives.

Chapter 10

Sexuality

Sex is generally understudied and overdramatized. It is a topic about which many of us are poorly informed. Paradoxically, it preoccupies our private dreams and hidden thinking. There is no single reality in life which has caused more foolishness and careless disregard for others. There is no subject about which so much has been written and spoken. And yet, we are still poorly informed.

For a long time those who spoke about sex approached the topic from the narrow viewpoint of its moral implications: is it right or wrong? how so and under what circumstances? Until recently, very little thought was given to the positive aspects of what sex should actually be, one of life's generous gifts, a tender subject deserving of sensitivity and respect. Even in our "modern" and more refined world, we find it difficult to be comfortable with the deeper meaning of sex, and we generally hide our embarrassment with the subject by vulgarity and humor. We sometimes attach guilt and shame to the topic, perhaps to avoid meeting it head-on, for the sake of understanding.

Obviously, sex and sexual expression are permanent features of human life. They enter the scene from the very beginning of history. We find the subject in every culture, every age, and there is always the effort to deal with it in some understandable way. Early mythology reveals our attempt to "sanctify" sex by showing that it engaged the time and energy of the gods themselves. It was the human way of saying that sexual feelings and needs went beyond the world and had something of the infinite and eternal about them, causing the same kind of puzzling joy and stress in the lives of the gods that they do in our own.

If you look at Scripture with a view to learning something about sex, you will find it there from the outset. Scripture says this: "It is not good for man to be alone. I will make a suitable partner. . . . That is why a man leaves his father and mother and clings to his wife, and the two of them become one body."

Jesus didn't speak a great deal about sex. It wasn't as important to him as some other subjects he wanted to address. But he did make some memorable statements about sex and the people who were having problems with it. He once told the lady caught in adultery that if no one else was going to accuse her, then he wasn't going to either. He told a prostitute that all the sins she'd ever committed could be forgiven because she loved much. He certainly didn't disapprove of sex. He was a guest at the marriage in Cana, which indicates that he saw the marriage contract as a normal aspect of living. He condemned adultery and lust, but really no more than he condemned hypocrisy, lying, or irreverence.

St. Paul told the Ephesians that marriage, and therefore presumably sexuality in marriage, was as close and intimate a union as the union of Christ to the church. He told the Corinthians that he preferred virginity, but that marriage was certainly acceptable. Sexuality isn't treated extensively in the Scriptures. There is certainly much in the Old Testament which we haven't mentioned, problems and foolishness of some of the people described there, the sins of normal people and their inability to always deal meaningfully with sex. But these sexual shortcomings are not presented as far more grave or blameworthy than their other sins. As a matter of fact, just the opposite is true. Sins of idolatry, breaking the covenant that God had given, and failure to obey God's commands were much more severely condemned. Concubines, mistresses, love trysts, and even several wives appear as acceptable.

In the early centuries of the church, sexuality is not a major topic of discussion. Some of the early church fathers mention the need for prudence and care, but there wasn't a detailed body of laws concerning the subject. Origen, an early theologian, expressed some ideas about sex being a problem and took a personal stance against it; but he was later censured by the official church for his radical approach. The state of women in that early period was a more prevalent subject: women were looked upon as inferior and sometimes seen as a danger to the superior male. The fourth century and St. Augustine marked a radical change in thinking about sexuality. Augustine was to set a new precedent, which has prevailed with far-reaching effect even to our own time.

St. Augustine, who was baptized a Christian, didn't take it all very seriously until some time later in his life. His early years were less than virtuous with a generous mixture of sexual experience. After his conversion, he reacted by being more than ordinarily rigid with regard to sex and its expression. Augustine had become a Manichean and thus believed that two supreme powers existed in the world, one evil and the other good. The supreme evil power was material and opposed to the supreme good power, which was spiritual. In keeping with these ideas, whatever was materially oriented, having to do with sensible realities, was evil. Therefore, sexuality, the use of sex, was looked upon as basically unacceptable. Even though Augustine later rejected this philosophy, the effects of these beliefs show up in his thinking and writing to the very end of his life.

It was out of this context that Augustine expressed his ideas about sexuality. He taught that sex was to be avoided at all cost and was the cause of much that is sinful and evil in us. He believed that sexual expression is a bad inclination in each of us. Avoiding such temptations is essential to the good Christian life. Sexual expression is permitted to married people, according to Augustine, but only for the express purpose of having children. That specific intention had to be present during every act of sex. If this intention wasn't there, the act became a matter of serious sin. To take pleasure in the act, even while intending to have children, was at least a venial sin. Augustine gives the strong impression that the world would be much better off without any sex at all, and that its only redeeming purpose is to offer some "safe" method of relieving our inclinations.

From the time of Augustine on, sex became a preoccupation with many theologians. Such great men as St. Jerome, St. Gregory the Great, and St. Bernardine of Sienna expressed totally negative attitudes toward sexuality. It is amazing to read some of the moral judgments made in those days. Women who died in childbirth were denied burial in consecrated ground. Any woman in her menstrual period could not receive communion. The need for sex was considered a kind of disease, a degradation of the person and always indecent. St. Gregory agreed that it was literally impossible to have intercourse without sin. Husbands and wives were counseled to abstain from intercourse for several days before receiving communion. Marriage was looked upon as a secondary state as compared to virginity and celibacy. St. Bernardine held that marriage was really the work of the devil. Monks and priests were strongly counseled to flee the company of women at all costs.

It is difficult to understand how these attitudes could have been accepted in the Christian world. It is perhaps reasonable to assume that all this theoretical teaching did not touch most of the people of the time. The point to be made is that we have certainly progressed beyond this early thinking, and we shouldn't assume now that the last word has been spoken about sex. If we think we know all there is to know about sexuality, then we need only look back at the "certitude" of those early figures who were so secure in what they were saying. They offer a lesson which should not be missed. If canonized saints in the church can be wrong, and they certainly were, it is quite possible that what we are teaching and advocating today might be subject to revision and further study.

We are never finished with sexuality. It is a reality which we have to continue to deal with, to clarify, with the hope of understanding more than we have so far. It can reasonably be said that we haven't been dealing very effectively with the subject, seeing that it still causes so much discomfort in so many lives. It is reasonable to project that none of us will ever be completely free of confusion and difficulty in our approach to sexuality. But at least we can diminish some of that confusion and difficulty by healthier, saner approaches.

Whenever we discuss sexual expression, our first question has always been whether it is right or wrong. How can we know the moral implications of sexuality? Are there cut and dried answers we can rely on? And, what is more important, can we live with those answers? Is sex good or bad? Is sex in my life good or bad? Is sex in marriage always morally good? Is sex outside of marriage always morally bad? On what do we base our answers? If there is less information than we had thought about the morality of sex in the Scriptures, can we be as sure as we always thought we were on the subject? Can we say that our present teachings are the correct and ultimate stand?

The answers to these questions are never simple. Let's consider an example or two. Suppose for a moment that a man and a woman meet in a bar. After a few drinks and conversation, they agree to spend the night together in a motel. There they freely engage in sexual activity. At the end of their time together, they politely thank each other and go their way, never to see each other again. Contrast that example with a couple who meet, date for an extended period of time, come to love each other, and mutually agree that because of their commitment and love, they are entitled to responsible sexual expression. Without making any moral judgments about either case, it is obvious that the same principles apply quite differently to each of them. Take another example of a wife who is unfaithful to her husband, who happens to be cruel and bullish, drinks too much, and approaches sex with insensitivity, concentrating only on his own needs and satisfaction. Once again, contrast that situation with the infidelity of the partner who sees sex as nothing more than a natural urge, something for pleasure and relaxation.

These examples should reveal that general principles concerning the morality of sexual expression are more difficult to determine than we might have thought. This doesn't mean that there are no principles, that we can approach sexuality from a totally unrestricted point of view. Neither does it mean that what we have held in the past is absolutely certain. It does mean that there should be better ways to determine the moral and good use of sexual expression. It might also mean that there would be times when we simply would not know for sure about the morality of a given sexual act. It is that unsureness which has always caused the greatest discomfort. That in itself might deserve more extensive consideration.

Can we say that there is a clear prohibition of certain sexual acts in the Old Testament? Is sex outside of marriage, for instance, clearly forbidden? The only concrete indication that any sexual expression is prohibited in the Old Testament is when it is seen as idolatrous or in the case of prostitution.

The sixth commandment given by God to Moses forbids adultery. Adultery is here considered to mean having sexual intercourse with someone other than one's married partner. In the past we have made much of how all sexual sins flow from that commandment, but a more realistic approach reveals that we have perhaps stretched the meaning of what the Mosaic law originally required.

The New Testament cannot be cited as simply condemning certain forms of sexual expression, in or out of marriage. As we have mentioned, it didn't seem to be uppermost in the mind of Jesus. We can certainly assume that Jesus, who had a great respect for the human person, would condemn sexual exploitation, a crude disregard for the person. It is obvious that much of what is accepted in the area of sex today would not be tolerated by Jesus. The free approach to any and all forms of sex which has become prevalent today, Jesus would surely condemn. Wife swapping, swinging single sexual relationships with no permanency or commitment, the selling of sexual substitutes in slick magazines with nude photos, and blatant promiscuity are clearly immoral. One could easily come to that conclusion without referring at all to what Jesus said.

But the questions about right or wrong are much more subtle and extend beyond these obvious examples.

Answers are much less apparent in the case of sincere and good people, who want to know what is right and do what is right but have the normal temptations to sexual activity. The New Testament says nothing about unavoidable sexual impulses, "bad" thoughts and masturbation, sexual expression flowing from deep love when marriage is temporarily impossible, birth control, desperate circumstances in marriage which block the possibility of meaningful sexual expression, and the whole range of problems which arise in puberty and adolescence. Again, this does not mean that because Jesus said nothing about these aspects of sexuality, we needn't either and are free to make uneducated judgments about them. It only means that we may reasonably question the certitude which had always been present in our approach to sexuality, as though we knew for certain and forever exactly what the morality of each sexual act was, regardless of circumstances and individual differences.

There is a subtle indication in our society that other people also have problems with sexuality. They have attempted to remedy this by the "sexual revolution." For many people, this represents a crude attempt to say that sex is good, so good that it can be brought out into the open, the marketplace, the theatre and literature, just about any place at all. The sexual revolution insists that we do away once and for all with outdated moral laws and prohibitions which we previously honored and revered. Many now look on sex as a natural biological function, something as natural as eating or sleeping, something for everyone without restriction or judgment.

If the sexual revolution seems overdone, it might be the natural swing of the pendulum from the opposite extreme of prudishness, seeing sex as evil and negative. This may be something we will just have to deal with for the time being. We might lament the fact that sex is used for every possible purpose, to express and seek approval, to bestow favor and appreciation. Sex is equated with love and even with passing affection. We have commercialized sex and use it to sell the strangest products, motor oil and shaving cream, somehow connecting them with sexual promise and pleasure. We give one another the impression that sexual adjustment will solve all of life's problems. Countless books have been written on sexual techniques, aids to compatibility, with the sure promise of sexual gratification. We like to give the impression that most people have found sexual utopias and that only a few have any problems with it. We still avoid admitting that there is a seamy side to distorted sex, and we hardly ever talk about the psychological voids in many people who try to fill their emptiness with disorganized and meaningless sexual expression. You might say that the sexual revolution certainly isn't a complete success, but it is forcing us to face some issues which we have ignored in the past.

One area where the so-called sexual revolution has been helpful is in determining more certainly what sex is not. After some years of greater liberty with regard to sex, we have come to some sane conclusions. Sexuality is not a fold-out photo of an anonymous nude with a smiling and beckoning face. Sensible people have come to recognize that the smile probably has more to do with what the body's owner is being paid for such a disarming pose. We have also learned other things. Sexuality is not a one-night stand, the happy culmination of the first date, the male conquest, the female seduction. We might think that those "powerful" experiences are the real thing, but they fade in significance and we eventually come to realize that we are trying to fill the gaps in security, identity, and acceptance with the wrong sort of thing. Indiscriminate sex too often neglects our real needs and fails to get us beyond the adolescent hope that the world will like us enough to approve us.

There are other things that sex is not. It solves no problems, it doesn't improve poor relationships, it doesn't make immature people mature, it doesn't make people with emotional problems emotionally sound. Sexuality is a quality which works best in wholesome people. Meaningful sexual expression occurs most naturally in persons who deal directly with life, are willing to risk something of themselves in their relationship with another, are considerate enough to want to give satisfaction to others. It might be said that balanced, whole people are able to make meaningful decisions about sex, enjoy its use, and are able to form deep and meaningful relationships which do not offer sexual expression. It could further be said that wholesome sexuality requires a full range of other personal qualities, many of which begin to develop long before sexual awakening.

There is still more we are coming to know. Marriage

doesn't necessarily legitimize sex. There can be as much
abuse of sexuality in marriage as outside it, and perhaps
more. Too often sexual expression becomes a means of
egotistic self-seeking rather than a way to serve the needs
of one's married partner. Sometimes sexual expression
becomes so commonplace that it hardly holds a place of
honor in marriage. Sex can become little more than a
common bodily function, with little regard for feelings or
needs. Men often perform the sexual act hurriedly and
matter of factly, as though it were an ordinary and routine
performance. Both men and women sometimes let former
guilt affect them, and they look upon sex as unclean,
something better omitted, better left to the young and
foolish. Sometimes one or other partner decides that sex
is no longer needed in their marriage, disregarding the
feelings of their spouse.

Still other observations can be made. As we mentioned, countless books with innumerable prohibitions
about sex have been written. Sex is the subject of sermons, retreats, spiritual renewals, and counseling ses-
sions, and is a constant visitor to the psychiatric couch.
In spite of all the laws, all the counsel and exhortation,
we seem to have slid backward rather than progressed.
At best, we might say that we have stood still. It is reasonable to ask why this is so. Will we ever overcome our
confusions and learn to live with ourselves, integrating
sexuality with healthy and conscientious expression?

Any answer to these questions must begin with a
question about the purpose of law. Does the law stand of
itself, or must it point to a clear value which it is pro-
tecting? The value which the law upholds should be evident to everyone who observes the law. To multiply laws
and to insist that some law cover every possible aspect
of sex only increases confusion and misunderstanding.
We are beginning to realize that this is exactly what we
have done in the past. Traditional textbooks on moral
theology have long chapters on sex dealing with the minutest details of thought and action, with corresponding

judgments about how sinful such acts are. The result is a feeling that sexuality is a negative thing and must be approached with greater caution than other human activity. Other virtues and vices at least seem less important. So once again, we find ourselves defining Christian life in terms of one aspect of it rather than seeing the whole picture.

Happily, we are approaching the subject of sex from a different point of view in recent times. We are talking less about individual sins and individual sex acts and more about attitude, regard for other persons, and a sense of respect for the meaning of sexuality. We are emphasizing values over the mere observance of law, and we are asking why the law demands what it does. In cases where the law seems vague and the value it is meant to uphold is not immediately apparent, we are asking whether the law should exist.

Let us take an example of a law concerning sexuality, asking whether the law is reasonable and whether the value the law upholds is clearly apparent. It is a law that sexual activity outside of marriage is always sinful, never permitted for any reason whatsoever. It is also a law that any sexual contact, even prolonged embracing or ordinary exchanges of affection which cause pleasure, are always sinful and, in most cases, seriously so. The logical implication of this is that love and respect have nothing to do with true sexual expression, only marriage. So long as one is married, even in the complete absence of love and respect, sexual expression is permitted and lawful. On the other hand, no matter the depth of love and the fullness of careful respect in an unmarried relationship, any sexual expression or pleasure is sinful. The basis for this law comes from the conviction of moralists who hold that sexual acts can only be responsibly performed in marriage. Yet many couples exhibit more responsibility outside of marriage than other couples do in marriage. It is perfectly clear that the law neglects a value which is most important, it might be said that there can never be meaningful sexual expression, in or out of marriage, without love and respect. To simply say that sexual expression in marriage is valuable and sexual expression outside of marriage is not valuable, is falling far short of what sexuality is meant to be. Most thinking persons would agree that sex outside of marriage is generally unsatisfactory, too often lacking in commitment, leaving the partners open to injury and personal pain. But all of these negative qualities can, and often do, exist in marriage. Perhaps it is time to begin speaking in terms of the human qualities which are necessary for meaningful sexual expression rather than continuing to speak of laws and sins.

Any sexual relationship must be founded on genuine care for another person. This means that one desires what is desired by one's partner, seeks to know him or her well enough to anticipate need, fulfill desire, and identify with the very thoughts and feelings of that person. We too often neglect such caring, sometimes entering a sexual encounter in the hope that it will produce care and concern. But ordinarily this does not happen. Caring for another must be studiously cultivated; it comes only as the result of effort and can only be undertaken when we value another person enough to want to care.

If we are committed to another, offering support for the sake of the relationship, we can say that we truly appreciate that person. That is, we value the good qualities in our partner so much that we want to assist in making them even better, richer. Sexual interchange cannot have meaning without appreciation of one's partner. Without this appreciation, sex becomes pragmatic and self-centered, what "I" want without regard for the needs of my partner.

Sexuality must always be responsible. It provides a setting in which two people must accept all the consequences of their actions. This responsibility is primarily directed toward one's partner, but secondarily and importantly, to the community. It means that the persons involved are aware of the expectations that are part of the relationship, what they are asking of each other, how they will manage the various effects which flow from their relationship. Such responsibility cannot be undertaken by those who do not understand the far-reaching consequences of sexuality, the need for care and appreciation.

One of the measures which can be applied to those who are giving themselves to one another has to do with the results of their relationship as seen by others. If there is no growth in a relationship, if it seems to stunt people and paralyze the development of human qualities, it can hardly be called meaningful. Many times it happens that, rather than bringing out the best in the couple involved, there is a kind of stagnation which arises from too much concentration on self, with no growth resulting. Another measure of a relationship has to do with the growth which the couple is able to foster in others. We can ask whether that is also apparent, or whether it is difficult to be around a couple because of their tensions, their concentration on each other, their selfish possession of "love."

Jesus urged us to be "pure in heart," assuring us that by being so we should see God. We have too often interpreted this to refer to the virtue of purity, avoiding sexual sins. A broader interpretation has to do with having good intentions and being open toward others. This quality is eminently applicable to sexual relationships. If we could honestly guarantee that our intentions were good toward others in dealing with them sexually, we would have no more need for laws about moral goodness and sexuality.

To summarize, then, any sexual relationship must presuppose certain features: commitment, care, appreciation, responsibly appropriate behavior, giving something good to the community, producing growth for the couple and for those around them. Obviously all these qualities cannot be present to a perfect degree in any relationship. But they are goals toward which we can strive, manifesting something of each of them in our approach to others. If these goals are seen as meaningful, and if they motivate us to use the necessary energy to realize them, we can say that personal relationships and sexual expression will be morally good.

It is difficult to promulgate laws to ensure these qualities. There is rather a tendency to see the law as unrelated to such values and as existing only for itself. We often see the law as the will of another, not understanding how it offers meaning to our own lives by our obedience to it. Obedience without understanding is devoid of meaning and gradually deteriorates to mere lip service. Perhaps this is why most people disregard the law unless there is a deeper conviction which speaks to what is nobler and more human in us. The only other method of upholding the law is through punishment, the threat of personal loss, and the imposition of guilt and shame.

In spite of all that people have said about sexuality, we have hardly begun. If we were willing to work at seeing the good in every individual, it would be hard to abuse the privilege of deep human relationships.

Let us go back to the beginning. What about sex? Is it right or wrong? Under what circumstances? Obviously there are no easy answers, and some things we thought were right and true in the past turn out to be less so in light of what we have seen. We have been talking more recently about the formation of conscience. That process always begins with gathering as much information as possible, then studying what has been said about the morality of a given act, weighing and balancing, and finally making a judgment. We know that sincere study and a conscientious effort to know the value of all the elements involved in a moral decision will lead us away from error rather than into it.

We are sometimes afraid that if we say "Let your conscience be your guide," everyone will choose evil, disregard what is good, and destroy the good order of things. We are not sure this will happen, but we assume so because we have become dependent on laws for everything we do. We live in an imperfect world, and we have to expect something of imperfection in life. But people are capable of good intentions, and sometimes we are better off when we offer one another the opportunity to make our own decisions.

With regard to sexuality, it is foolish to suggest that everyone should make his or her own decisions about how to act. But to motivate ourselves to gather information, to study, to confer with others, to strive always to be sincere and keep the needs of others in clear perspective, seems more meaningful than to simply rely on laws which others have devised. One thing is certain, even though we must continue to struggle, the results are worth the effort.

Chapter 11

Liturgy

Imagine the scene at the Last Supper. The setting was simple, an upper room prepared for dining, no special furniture, the regular features of that day. Jesus and the apostles were gathered informally around a table. Words such as "reclining" and "seated" are used to describe the casual atmosphere. The guests talked freely with one another; they sometimes directed their remarks to Jesus, the acknowledged "leader" of the ceremony, but they also spoke to those nearby, murmuring asides and comments. There was a certain informality about the occasion. As it is described in the gospels, it was a gathering of friends who knew one another well enough to be comfortable and at ease together.

There was a specific ritual connected with the supper, but it was not so rigid that it did not admit of some variations. It was rather a framework within which spontaneity was possible. Certain prayers were offered. Some songs were sung, and the story was told of the delivery of the Jewish people from Egypt and their entry into the Promised Land, from slavery to freedom. Those present ate specially prepared foods and drank wine at specific intervals; these were symbols used to illustrate the story as it was told by the narrator.

At the Last Supper Jesus made a dramatic departure from the traditional meal when he gave bread and wine to the apostles, telling them that these were his body and blood and that they should remember his presence among them by reenacting this scene. There was nothing absolutely sacred or unchangeable about that last and "first" meal, except the command to "remember" Jesus in the breaking of the bread and the passing of the cup. The language, the setting, the furnishings, the clothes, and the people present were to change drastically and repeatedly in years to come. To single out vestments or language, or to say that furnishings or songs, or certain gestures had to be present for the ceremony to be complete, would be inaccurate. We might go even further by saying that a ceremony could be letter-perfect, with the right vestments, language, furnishings, and quiet atmosphere of a "liturgically" appropriate church, and yet could be all wrong for its lack of warmth and friendship. On the other hand, a ceremony among friendly and willing people, bound together by mutual regard and love, clearly speaks the presence of Jesus, regardless of all the secondary features about style and ritual.

This is certainly the way it was in the early church. There were simple gatherings in which the people came together "for the breaking of the bread," a time for informal celebration when the presence of Jesus was keenly felt. There was no *set* procedure, nothing to which the participants had to adhere, as though the "remembering" of Jesus could not take place without it. The only requisite mentioned by St. Paul was worthiness: persons were not to participate unless they were determined to "proclaim the death of the Lord until He comes." As a matter of fact, the setting of the ceremony was always changing; sometimes it preceded a regular family meal, sometimes it followed it, sometimes it was done by itself. Jesus gave no commands as to how the Last Supper was to be reenacted.

Let us pass then from imagination to fantasy. Just suppose, first of all, that one of the apostles played the guitar and "happened to bring it along." We add a variation by singing a few new songs. Suppose that Peter had invited his family, and his wife insisted on dancing, endeavoring to recall some of the emotions of the Jews while they were in slavery. Peter's mother-in-law had volunteered to bake the bread. (Someone certainly baked it. Who was it?) Two of the apostles made a banner to hang behind the table; the banner read: "This is the bread come down from heaven." Another apostle had written a little poem which he hoped to read about what Jesus had said in the Sermon on the Mount, and what the disciples had gotten out of it, how it had changed their lives, and how they were grateful. Finally, a woman there gave everyone a beautiful flower because flowers signify the new life which is always coming into the world, symbols of the life that Jesus had given them when he told them they were of much more value than the lilies of the field.

It might be certain that none of these features were present at the Last Supper. It is even a little ridiculous to talk as if they were. But, there is a deeper observation we can make. If they had existed, would we have to say that the supper was essentially different? Is it possible that the presence of Jesus could not have been there because of these changes? With a little thought, we can see that the setting is less important than the presence of Jesus at the ceremony. If music and dance, some readings and friendly gestures could improve the setting and make it more attractive for the people there, who could say that these "changes" were unacceptable?

Liturgy has traditionally been defined as the "official prayer of the church." There are certain times when the whole community of believers comes together to pray. The church is made up of all the members who believe. We have often thought that the "official" church is the pope and bishops and clergy. A better definition embraces every member of the Christian community. This community of believers prays together at Mass, at the sacraments, at ceremonies of various kinds, and whenever two or three are gathered together in the name of Jesus. If a parish community were to have a prayer service for the sick, it could be called a "liturgy." If they attend a marriage, a baptism, the blessing of a new home, or say a prayer in time of drought, these are all liturgies.

The principal liturgical ceremony in the church is the Mass, when the whole community gathers to remember the presence of Jesus among them at the Last Supper, the time when Jesus assured his followers of his continuing life in their midst.

Every liturgy involves some sort of ceremony. We use things that we can see and touch and feel, things which help us express what our prayer is saying. We might use candles to signify our belief in Jesus as the light of the world, and our effort to be lights also. We sometimes use incense to symbolize how our prayer rises to God, the offerings of previous times are now replaced by the living sacrifice of Jesus. A gold chalice might remind us that we are doing very special things at Mass. A white baptismal garment symbolizes the new life in the Christian community. The washing of feet on Holy Thursday shows our willingness to serve one another, just as Jesus served us and told us that service was essential to the Christian life.

In every liturgical action, we are concerned with two things: what the ceremony is saying and how we can say it best. For example, the ceremony of baptism says that the parents and the community are resolved to share their faith in Jesus with the child by teaching and example. We say this best by using symbols, material objects, gestures, and actions which express and confirm our intentions. We use oil, symbolizing the strength and health which the Christian faith will give the child. We use light to signify the light of Christ which will direct and enlighten the way for the new Christian. We use a baptismal robe to express the new life which comes in baptism. Finally, we use water to show continuing life, the quenching of spiritual thirst, the pure life which can be achieved in the Christian community.

What the ceremony says does not change. How we can say it best not only can change, but should do so, so that it can be better understood and appreciated. For example, the ceremony of the Mass, the supper which Jesus gave us, will always say that Jesus is present among us in the breaking of the bread. It happens that using a vernacular language rather than Latin helps to convey the message more effectively, at least for most of the community. The use of contemporary music which speaks to us "where we are" may help us better understand what the ceremony is saying. While we firmly believe that Jesus is present among us, it may be that we can express this best by relaxing a little, being friendly with one another in church, and even by exchanging some conversation before the ceremony begins. In these ways we can learn that Jesus was a friendly and conversational person.

One of the major problems of liturgy today centers around a confusion between what the ceremony is saying and how best to say it. In many cases, we have acted as though the way we express the message is more important than the message itself. The vestments, music, language, gestures, and specific prayers have sometimes become more important than the underlying reality of it all. We often add to this confusion by calling these features "sacred tradition," intimating that they cannot change. To insist that language, gestures, music, or anything else could never change would be like insisting that nothing new could be added to medical science, or to the art forms of painting or sculpture. It is only reasonable to expect that liturgy, the official prayer of the believing community, could become more effective, and better express our essential beliefs about the Christian life.

A phrase we have been using recently, "liturgical reform," expresses the idea of adapting liturgy so that it speaks more effectively to the needs and thinking of our own age. Liturgical reform comes from the conviction that there are always better ways to pray, to worship, and to strengthen our Christian belief. As the world changes to embrace new ideas and discoveries, greater population, technology and mechanization, better education, expanded awareness through books, movies, and other media, liturgy should help us to express what we are feeling about these things and how they all fit into our belief and prayer. To live as if none of these things existed would be to ignore the purpose of liturgy in our lives.

So, liturgical reform continues to ask questions about how we can pray most meaningfully and whether we understand our everyday lives in light of the Christian message. Through liturgical reform we evaluate, refine, and update ceremonies, prayers, music, vestments, and language—literally everything we use in liturgy.

Let's take an example. It was a long-standing custom in the church to use black vestments for the Mass of burial. This practice came from our former emphasis on the sadness of death and judgment, a warning to the living to reform their lives. There was less reflection on the idea of Jesus' resurrection and the promise of salvation for those who believe. With the passage of time, however, and a deeper appreciation of God's mercy and forgiveness and less fear of punishment, we "reformed" the older custom by using white vestments. We began celebrating the Mass of the resurrection, rather than the requiem. This liturgical reform came about because of the insights offered by those who see death as an integral part of life, not a final punishment. Here is a case where liturgical reform was welcomed by most people as a positive movement away from the depressing symbols of hopelessness which we had too often connected with death.

Here's another example we might consider. The

music at most liturgies was customarily played on the organ, the majestic instrument of religion and formality. On certain occasions, such as Christmas and other special feasts, we might have heard a violin, perhaps a cello. At times of great solemnity, ceremonies in which the pope or high dignitaries participated, trumpets were used for triumphal marches and entries. The highest liturgical song was always Gregorian chant, developed in early monasteries and passed on, sometimes with great effectiveness, to the people. These forms of music and chant were happily received by many as expressive and beautiful. In recent times, however, organ music has become less attractive than it was in the past, at least for many people. Gregorian chant, while beautiful when properly sung, is not easily mastered without much practice and repetition. Liturgical reform is asking us to consider the music of our own time. Is there something absolutely sacred about the organ or Gregorian chant? Can we replace them with something more expressive of our own time and circumstances? Can different kinds of music help us get in touch with our needs and feelings? The use of other instruments, the guitar for example, popularized by folk music and ballads, the flute, percussion and rhythm ensembles, and even bands and orchestras, are all an effort to bring what is meaningful and pleasing into our religious outlook and practice. This does not mean a complete rejection of the organ or Gregorian chant so much as an addition of other forms of musical expression which are pleasing to many people. Neither does it mean that modern liturgical music is better. Obviously at times it is mediocre, words and lyrics which are a brave failure at rhyming and say too little. Transitions are seldom smooth. But one thing is certain; there is more participation in the congregations today, and a deeper sense of belonging than there has been for a long time.

Nothing by its nature is unholy. The organ is not holier than the guitar; Gregorian chant is no more sacred than a modern hymn written by a liturgical composer. It is the intention and the aspiration involved that count. We can make the most sacred things common and vulgar. And we can sanctify the most ordinary things in our lives.

Liturgical reform has not only touched requiems and the kind of music we sing and play at Mass. It has swept across every aspect of the liturgy. With a few exceptions, we are seeing much that is different in churches today, as contrasted with just a few years ago. At Mass, for example, we find the priest much more closely engaged with the people, facing them, encouraging participation and even dialogue. Many more people are directly involved in the ceremony itself: readers, ministers of communion, musicians, commentators, ushers to greet the people and make them feel a part of what is happening. In most churches the congregation is at least attempting to sing. All of this is a new and different experience which demands adjustment. One might hear the members of the congregation praying spontaneously. There is more awareness of the theme that runs through the liturgy of a particular Mass; there is a new emphasis on how the readings might apply to daily living. In most churches you will find the people friendly, interested, willing to converse, and even socializing before and after the service. These are just a few of many liturgical reforms which have contributed to better and more personal ceremonies.

In addition to the Mass, liturgical reform has touched every sacrament: marriage, baptism, penance, anointing of the sick, confirmation, and ordination. In each case there has been a new effort toward deeper understanding, with emphasis on what is required of those who are to receive the sacraments. Simpler prayers have been written for the ceremonies with an effort to signify that they are a part of daily life, not far removed from what is practical and ordinary.

Many people have welcomed the changes in the liturgy. If liturgy can speak to our lives and help us to see the connection between prayer and living, it adds a much-needed dimension to what religion should be.

In the past, it was quite possible to attend Mass, receive the sacraments and assist at devotions, sometimes for years, even a lifetime, without ever feeling a sense of kinship with the other people who were doing the same thing. It was possible to sit next to other parishioners in the same pew, to see the same people Sunday after Sunday, and yet never speak to them or even acknowledge that we had seen them before. It is still quite possible to do all this in today's liturgically reformed church. But it's a bit more difficult, and there's always the danger that someone will approach us and urge us to participate in some way.

On the other side of the coin are those who have resisted change and hold that the reform has already caused too much trouble and confusion, and we should have left the church the way it was. Our troubles began when we started changing things that were right for the church during all those previous centuries. How can the church change so much? Does this mean that we were wrong in the past? When will the changes end? Isn't it against the will of God, and didn't Jesus give us everything we needed for our belief and religious practice?

These are grave questions and should not be dismissed lightly, as if those asking them were unenlightened or too stubborn to listen and understand. Because the church was in an apparently stable condition for such a long time and so many changes took place in such a short time, it is understandable that many would be concerned and confused. Perhaps we can offer a few thoughts to diminish this concern.

To begin with, the notion of change itself deserves clarification. Can the church change? Can liturgical ceremonies change? Change can occur, and as a matter of fact it has occurred throughout the history of the church. In liturgy, as we mentioned, we are always seeking better ways to express our faith through prayer and worship. It is not the truths which change, the presence of Jesus in the breaking of the bread, for example, but rather the way we express the truth. Husbands and wives might love each other throughout life. Their love should grow even stronger with the passage of time. Ideally, they will always be seeking new ways to show their love to one another. The love itself doesn't change. It remains stable because of a deep appreciation of the other person. But a dynamic and living love will always be expressing itself in new and more graphic ways. Liturgy is an expression of what we believe about God and our relationship to God. Liturgy looks for ways to express this effectively and with conviction.

Another comment we can make with the hope of shedding light on the resistance many people have to liturgical change has to do with security and the blessings of stability. Most of us who are older can remember times in the past when life seemed to be simpler, less demanding, more peaceful and predictable. Even young persons sometimes speak of the past as a better time. There is a general feeling of nostalgia in our time, a harking back to "what was" as better than "what is." Perhaps this longing backward glancing is characteristic of every age. Whatever the explanation, it is a matter of fact that we often think of the past as more comfortable than the present or the future. Because life often gets to be too much for us, we long for what seems more secure.

It is natural that our religious outlook and practice would be related to this kind of thinking. As we look back to those times of stability and security, our religion stands out as the most stable element. But then the church began to change. Old and dependable signs of its stability began to disappear, particularly in the areas of liturgy. We could not be as certain as we always had been. It was impossible to keep up with the changes in the Mass and the sacraments. One week, English was used. Only a few weeks later, the priest began facing the people. He no longer whispered the sacred words of the canon, but spoke them out loud and boldly. Readers began to appear. We were told to sing. Unashamedly guitars were brought in; choirs were moved from the loft to the front of the church. It never seemed to end. Everything changed. Where churches were peaceful and quiet places, houses of prayer and meditation, all kinds of activities began to take place. People laughed and talked there and seemed disrespectful of so much that had been taught. At the same time, old reliable religious practices began to disappear. Gone the Tuesday novena, benediction on Saturday evenings, devotions and services of various kinds. There was too much going on with too little explanation.

If we look deeply enough to distinguish the essentials from what is accidental to religion, we will still find the basics, unchanged and absolutely certain. It is just possible that we are more certain of some truths now than we have been at any other time in history. Jesus came to announce the good news of God's concern for each of us. He insisted that we be unafraid, at peace, confident that we have been accepted by God, who cares for us without limit. He further insisted that we are worthy, that we have dignity, and that we can find the good that God has offered to each of us. It is the responsibility of liturgy to find ways to express all that, to celebrate what is joyful and meaningful in life, and to support us with God's assurance, expressed through Jesus, that life is always meaningful and good.

If we look deeply enough, we will find that liturgy had become somber and somewhat irrelevant to life in the world where we live. It had lost the joy which should come from knowing that, whatever our sorrow, it shall be turned into rejoicing; that, if God is for us, who can be against us? If change is necessary to better express these marvelous and unchanging truths, we need understanding rather than rejection, acceptance rather than emotional nostalgia.

There is no better way to end this chapter than by considering what liturgists are recommending for a deeper appreciation of ceremony and ritual in our lives. These considerations will underlie future change and renewal.

Liturgy is, first of all, a celebration, something we

have not always remembered. It should be a happy coming together of the community, a thankful and joy-filled acknowledgment that we are gifted and that no one in the community need be in want. The earth is ours. Moreover, God has spoken to us through Jesus, assuring us that we are called to the kingdom, which is like a precious treasure.

If you watch a football game or attend a neighborhood party, you become aware that joy and celebration are possible. On these occasions people are uninhibited and freely engage in the kind of exchanges which foster good feelings. There is a certain ritual they follow, cheering for victory, eating food, conversation, identification with the "heroes" of the game. The important realities have less to do with the "ritual" than with the feeling of the persons there who are entering into it. There are spontaneous reactions: singing, shouting, clapping of hands; but these are not so structured that everyone is doing them on signal.

If you contrast such "liturgies" with the Mass, for example, you will find that much is needed to achieve even a little of the naturalness of other settings. Our thinking about Mass has often focused on getting in and out as quickly as possible, so we can get on with the business of living. We even talked humorously about priests who said the Mass faster and how we hoped we could "hit" that Mass to get out sooner. In many churches there is very little spontaneity, and we often look upon such "outbursts" as disorderly. "Remember, you are in church." There has been too much preoccupation with "getting it right." We used to spend hours drilling altar boys with the time of genuflections, bows, the position of the hands, the procedures of moving the book and ringing the bells. We gave the impression that such disciplines were really the important matter of liturgy.

The aspects of joy and celebration gave way to military discipline, rigid adherence to a structure. We are now beginning to relax and see all that as far less important than having people at ease, happily acknowledging the presence of Jesus among them, and feeling God's spirit at work in the way they welcome and accept one another.

Good liturgy requires interest in every person at the celebration. This must be primary, the assurance that we are carrying out the command of Jesus to love one another. Too often newcomers to parishes complain that it is hard to "break in," and sometimes one may remain an "outsider" for years. This might come from viewing liturgy as ceremony which exists for its own sake, without involving those present. Such a notion must be replaced with a warm regard for flesh and blood people. We must not view liturgical ceremonies as we might view an art exhibit, looking and enjoying, but never letting anything happen to us personally. A parish is healthy in proportion to the personal regard the people have for one another. The one place this interest and regard can be measured is at the liturgy.

We do not come to "find Jesus" at liturgy. We come to celebrate the fact that we have discovered Jesus "out there" in our daily lives. Because of that discovery, we can come together to joyfully acknowledge that we are able to make Jesus present in the bread because we have made him present in what we do, because we have "seen him" in the least suspected places and people. We come rich with his presence in us and say to the community that we are worthy to receive him in the bread because we have long since made a place for him in our lives, the place we give to our neighbors, our family, workers at the factory, and even our enemies. Without this effort, liturgy is an empty ritual, like saying we love someone when we are really filled with careless indifference.

Parishes used to have more devotions and services: benediction, novenas, missions, and home devotions. But because much of this became empty, ritual for ritual's sake, we are finding far less of these in our lives. There is a great need for alternate liturgies. These will, hopefully, develop as we learn that we are capable of praying in family settings, that we can make something more of our meals together, celebrate birthdays and anniversaries in religious settings, and seek new ways of expressing our faith and confidence in God. These will be steps toward richer and more satisfying liturgical celebrations.

Let us end as we began, in imagination and fantasy. Picture a parish of about two hundred families. At certain times of liturgical celebration, not always at Mass, not always with a priest, the people begin to gather, some time ahead of the appointed hour. There is genial conversation and an effort to get to know one another. The atmosphere is warm and friendly and joyful. The ceremony is relaxed, a time of restful well-being. The service fits readily into the lifestyle of those present. They have prepared for this liturgical celebration by living out their Christian lives in work and play. Being there is natural, the direct consequence of living in a Christian setting.

A long way to go, you say? Indeed. But achievement is measured by progress toward the goal, not by arriving at the goal itself. It is intention which is important, the desire to reform what is in need of change. The best thing would be for us to arrive at that goal; the worst, that we would fall short of it, but we would still be ahead of what has become outmoded and paralyzed.

Chapter 12

Prayer

Someone once told a story about a five year old who was staying for a time with her grandparents. Even though the old folks were second generation, they usually spoke German with each other around the house. On a given evening the little girl was fervently saying her prayers, asking for this and that, imploring blessings on various members of the family. Toward the end of her prayer, she drew a long breath and sighed heavily. Then she said, "And please, God, help me to understand Grandma and Grandpa."

The sincere pleading of the child startled her grandmother who immediately spoke to Grandpa. Depending on one's point of view, this could be seen as an immediate answer to prayer, perhaps even a miracle in the eyes of the child. One reason this story might be significant is that we all wish prayer were just that simple.

But it isn't, as most of us have admitted at one time or another. Indeed, we may have spent a lot of time trying to understand prayer and trying to get some perspective on it for ourselves.

It is much easier to define prayer than to understand how it works in our lives. From long ago we have heard that prayer is raising the mind and heart to God. There is an even shorter formula: Prayer is talking with God. But deep down we have to admit that the definitions are only words, and they might leave us as mystified as ever about what really happens when we pray.

We have often settled for definitions and descriptions given to us by others, those we were told were experts in the field. People like St. Theresa of Avila and St. John of the Cross wrote long treatises about prayer, kinds of prayer, and how to become more effective at it. There is no shortage of authors on the subject; they address themselves to the complex notions of active and contemplative prayer, formal and spontaneous, and new forms replacing the old.

But efforts to define prayer have always fallen short of our expectations. To say that prayer is praising God or thanking the Lord and Creator for all he has given us is helpful and motivating. To define prayer further as expressing sorrow for our sins or asking God for what we need assures us that prayer is desirable in our lives. But there is obviously more. There must be some way to sense God's presence in our daily lives as natural and in harmony with every event as it unfolds.

That we want to pray is obvious. There is so much in each of us which we only partially understand. Who of us has not stood in the face of mystery, some unexplainable reality, and been at a loss to describe our feelings or to express our reactions in a meaningful way? On dark nights, in the center of a quiet forest, at the setting of the sun, in deep conversations, at times of awakening love, birth, death, and in thousands of other personal events, we feel a presence, something far beyond us, and we can only hope for some kind of continuing contact with that transcending reality. Whatever those good experiences may be, we long for them and relish their presence when they do visit us.

If we cannot satisfactorily define prayer, we can at least add some meaningful shades to existing definitions. To pray is to center our entire hope in God. We are always experiencing an attraction toward something beyond ourselves. We long to be what we have not yet become. We aspire to goals which demand more of us than we have thus far given. We want more from life than we have thus far received. We want to love and be loved, to give of ourselves freely. We want to accomplish, succeed, conquer. We are always longing for what might be, looking around the corner, waiting for tomorrow. We hope that such longings and ambitions are not neurotic, as can happen in our scattered world. But however undefined that pulling might be, prayer should mean that we are centering that entire energy and direction in God. Prayer is an expression of belief that God gives us whatever we need to fulfill those hopes and is always helping us to bring our intense longings to reality.

Prayer is not restricted to fervent believers, of course. It is part of our nature to pray whether or not we are consciously aware of it. In whatever way we are struggling to do good, we are praying, at least in the sense of admitting there are powers or forces beyond ourselves. Christian prayer simply means that we consciously admit our dependence on God to bring about what is best in us.

The way we pray is subject to change, and not everyone prays in the same way. Fundamentally, human needs are much the same. Our longings are similar to those who have gone before us. But the approach we make to prayer suits our needs and inclinations. Jesus prayed in a way that was characteristically Jewish. The prayer of St. Francis was different from that of Jesus. And our prayer is quite different from that of Jesus and St. Francis.

Sometimes we lament the changes that have come about in our prayer. We remember pictures of families gathered together after a meal or kneeling in prayer in the evening. The rosary was often said in those days or some other prayers which could be said in unison. Private prayer followed much the same pattern. In church or in one's room, the repetition of formulas written by holy people were quite acceptable and fit well into our notion of prayer. With most prayerful people there was a strong belief that the more time spent at prayer, the better it was. To spend an hour in prayer was better than half that time. The more one prayed, somehow, the holier that person was assumed to be.

Admittedly, there is less formal prayer now in the lives of most Catholics than there has been in the past. Many do not recite prayers at all. If we lament the passing of these practices, it should be because they have not been replaced with something sound and positive. If we have dropped the rosary, novena prayers, devotional formulas, and prayer books, we might legitimately ask whether we have replaced them with something which fulfills our need to pray. We might agree that many older ways of praying are no longer meaningful. But instead of finding more satisfactory methods, many people have simply given up prayer, or at best, are vague about what role it plays in their lives.

These thoughts bring us to a consideration of prayer in modern times. What's new in prayer? Do people still pray? How?

Without disregarding the practical aspects of prayer as most of us have known them, we have seen some healthy directions developing in the past twenty years. No one would claim to have determined once and for all what prayer should be. Most would agree that we still have much to learn about its meaning. But we can confidently assert that the practice of prayer has not been neglected in our times.

Formerly, many of us might have assumed that real prayer was only for a select few. These were deeply spiritual people, mostly in convents and monasteries, who had a high calling and spent most of their time delving into the mysteries of the spiritual life. The rest of us felt that we only dabbled in the outer precincts and would never become truly people of prayer. We shunned words which signified expertise: contemplation, the prayer of union, meditation, and the illuminative way. We could honor those who did this, but it was clearly not for us. Others would have to satisfy whatever "need" God had for this kind of prayer.

Gradually, we have revised our thinking and have gained some confidence about our own ability to pray. We have come to believe that prayer might not be so difficult as we might have been led to believe by the experts. We are bolder now and acknowledge that we are quite capable of praying, and as a matter of fact we do pray in many ways. We are becoming more comfortable with the notion that prayer is natural, a spontaneous flowing of deep sentiment from our inner selves. To admire the beauty of the mountains and see them as God's gracious creation is prayerful indeed. It might well be said that frantic efforts to pray within the limits of words and the rejection of distractions might make us miss the mountains altogether. To enjoy a deep conversation with a friend, to relish the well chosen words of a poem, or to have a deep appreciation for the gift of life, might all be missed if we kept too closely to what we were told prayer ought to be.

Spontaneity and joy are some new ingredients which have been added to prayer in recent times. Formerly, prayer was always a little sad, tight-lipped, and unsmiling. The newer response of joy might come from our need to celebrate life in a world where much is sad and uncertain. We are too aware that tomorrow is only a promise, and the future of the world seems to be out of our control. Wars, violence, the threat of total destruction, and the loss of peace are shadows which constantly darken our horizon. We need joy in our lives. We need joyful prayer which will stand up against so much which is somber and deadly serious. In these days it is prayer indeed to laugh and celebrate the richness of a certain moment, a bird's song, or the smile of a child. It is a prayer which expresses the deep hope we have that a new day will dawn.

Charismatics and spirit-filled people want to free themselves from old restrictions and inhibitions. They feel compelled to shout out praise to the God who is in them, healing, consoling, and speaking through them. Whereas in times past, prayer was a rather quiet affair between oneself and God, it has become public, shared by all, spoken in tongues and prophecy and interpretation. While we might not fully understand these approaches to prayer, we can hope that they are a source of satisfaction and peace to those who practice them. To pray in openness and with joyful spirits seems somehow better than to pray with long faces and the perverse notion that painful prayer is better.

Other developments which might help us to understand prayer speak of God's response to us when we pray. Traditionally we have believed that God listens to us and will answer our prayers and give us what we ask. Jesus said that we could ask anything of God and it would be done. He added that what was needed and was too often missing was faith. With the right kind of faith we could hurl mountains into the sea and do even greater things than he did. He said that if we ask, we can expect to receive, like knocking on doors and asking for what we need.

We have always struggled with this assurance which Jesus offers. Did he actually mean to say that God is waiting to hear our prayer and responds accordingly? Will God give us what we want no matter the cost or consequence?

Many theologians interpret what Jesus said as meaning that we can be confident that God has done great deeds in all of us and that as a people we have everything we need for life. What we are asking of God has already been accomplished. When we pray for something, to pass a test or to find a good husband, we are reminding ourselves that God has given us everything we need to effect what we are asking. We know it would be unreasonable to ask to pass a test if we hadn't studied. Someone has said that prayer doesn't change God, it rather changes us. If this is true, then prayer does accomplish miraculous effects.

We might take that line of thinking a step further by talking about prayer and the community. Let us suppose that someone is sick and we are praying for the person to recover. Our prayer is an admission that we are willing to do whatever we can to minister to the sick person. In a real sense, then, God has answered our prayer. If we pray for old people, the poor, or the hungry, we are implying that we will do everything in our power to respond to the needs of these people. When these things happen, it is a miracle, like hurling mountains into the sea and doing even greater things than Jesus did. The answer which God gives to those who are sick is doctors, nurses, hospitals, and medical technology. The answer God gives to the poor who pray for relief is the rich person who is asked to give out of the excess which he enjoys. All too often it is we, not God, who refuse to answer prayer. We can choose to remain insensitive to the needs of others, to turn away and refuse to give others what God has so generously given to us.

Does all this mean to say that God never intervenes, never actually changes the course of events in response to those who are praying and those who are in need? Can we pray for rain in time of drought, for peace in a fractured world, or that our team will win? There are some things we have no control over and regardless of how much we would like to change them, in some cases we cannot. Can we ask God to fill in where we are deficient?

These are difficult questions indeed, and they stand at the very heart of what prayer means. The Scriptures say that it has not yet been revealed to us what we shall be. That might mean that we have powers within us which haven't begun to be tapped. Sometimes we hear of marvelous feats, incredible accomplishments by people who cannot explain how it all happened. We know that most of us have psychic forces whose power surfaces only rarely, if at all. We also know that believing that something can happen is somehow essential to freeing forces within ourselves so that it can happen. Jesus often asked people for faith so that what they were asking could be accomplished. There is much matter for consideration here and no room for glib answers. Prayer must always remain something of a mystery. It is difficult to say what could happen in a community if it concentrated fully on accomplishing what God has invited us to experience.

To say that God never intervenes in the affairs of people presumes too much. We can only say that it is not impossible for God to change the course of events. Perhaps it is better to acknowledge that God is here with us, present in what we do, always accomplishing good with us and through us as we act in accord with what is asked of us.

Prayer should never be a tranquilizer, a dodge in which we simply leave everything to God. It would be meaningless to pray for the poor, the sick, those who are persecuted, and then expect God to take care of their problems. Perhaps we have done too much of that in our Christian lives. To expect God to do more than has been done already is meaningless. It is better not to pray at all than to pray in such a detached and unsympathetic manner. Prayer is a clear admission that we are willing to become involved, to do our part. It is giving witness that we have found the treasure and are willing to open it up to others. We should at least be cautious about throwing ourselves into prayer in order to avoid seeing the needs of those around us. We sometimes tend to rationalize that God needs our prayers and cannot get along without them. We sometimes get the notion that if we stop repeating the name of God, God might forget us. Hopefully we are beginning to get better ideas in this regard.

The gospel writers emphasized that Jesus was a prayerful person. Matthew recalls that he began his public life with a retreat in the wilderness where he fasted and prayed for forty days and nights. John records that the events at the end of his life were integrated with deep prayer. Before the events of his passion and death, Jesus went to the garden of Gethsemane to pray for strength. He prayed before other important events like the choosing of the apostles. The writers also note that at special times he "sliped away" to pray.

We can draw several conclusions from this effort to portray Jesus as sensing the need for prayer in his own life. By his example he expressed the natural inclination all persons experience for prayer. If we bear in ourselves the image of Jesus, we must each become prayerful in our own right. Even though the mode of our prayer might change to better accommodate our times, prayer itself can never be abandoned or relegated to a secondary place in Christian life.

We must admit here at the end of this chapter that we have not answered the long-standing question, what is prayer? But at least we can say there are some characteristics which are common to prayer in every age. While we might not use the same prayers or style of praying as others have in the past, prayer itself should still be very much a part of our lives. We would miss something vital if we thought we were being very modern and sophisticated and, therefore, no longer needed to pray.

Certain features of prayer, then, have become more widely recognized in our days than in the past. We would say those people are prayerful who are sensitive to what is happening around them. Perhaps they see more. They are attuned to the realities of their lives and their relationships to God; they grasp what is deeply present in the world which speaks of the transcendent. They are persons who are reverent in the face of mystery, the overwhelming majesty of life. They can feel and appreciate God's presence in what is apparently ordinary and everyday, but which for them has become very special. They speak to God with easy familiarity. They might choose to use formal words; they feel comfortable praying with others. But there is a readiness in them to be spontaneous, informal. For them prayer does not begin and end at specific times. It is a way of life, an attitude which endures and permeates whatever they do. Prayerful people are sensitive and discerning. Hopefully, we are among them.

There is something especially beautiful about the experience of prayer. Perhaps it has to do with the feeling of security and well-being we have when we pray. To be dependent upon someone outside of ourselves and at the same time to know that that person cares for us, wants good for us, is a powerful consolation. We like those feelings, and when we pray, we ask ourselves why we don't pray more and make more time for it. We resolve to be less "busy" and reserve a part of our day for enough quiet to let prayer happen to us.

We like to remember times of innocence in our youth when we prayed with fervor and childlike faith. We can easily relate to the little girl who asked God to help her understand her grandparents. We wish we could still sense something of that candor in ourselves, but we lament the fact that somehow life turned out to be less than we thought.

It might just be possible to return, at least to a sense of faith and trust in God's care for us. After going off into dark and remote corners of life, and often after less than satisfying experiences, people do come back to prayer. They find it pleasing. Witness the young people who long to pray and experiment in meditation, mantras; they need something that is permanent. Witness those who find peace amidst the stress and tensions of busy lives.

The clear message which prayer should give to each of us is simply that it is possible to touch and appreciate what is beyond ourselves. If at any time in our lives, in spite of fracture and crisis, we could say, "My soul magnifies the Lord . . . the mighty has done great things in me," it is enough. We might not use the same words, but somehow we will be expressing the same or similar ideas. That is prayer.

Chapter 13

Mary and the saints

If you asked a high school boy what he knew about St. Francis of Assisi, he most likely would be hard put to say very much. The same would probably be true if you asked a young girl about St. Catherine of Siena. As a matter of fact, the same might well be true for most of us. We might be able to give a few vague details about some of the saints, but probably not too much depth and background. Even if someone asked us about Mary, our knowledge might be limited to a few devotional notions, that she was the mother of Jesus, has been given some important titles, and has been very highly regarded in the Catholic church.

Going back to the high school students, if you asked them who won last year's academy awards or who were the last three winners of the super bowl, you could expect to get some more accurate information. In fact, not only would you likely get clear answers, but you would get a wealth of additional information about the subjects also.

A lot might be said about these responses and what is really important to today's Catholic people. We might wonder why persons who have been so specially recognized—saints, holy men and women—have come to be all but forgotten. We might ask whether the saints will ever become important to us again. Did they fill a need which no longer exists? What was their purpose anyway?

One thing is for sure, we all need heroes, models, or examples on whom to model our lives. The reason for that is simple. Great people of the past and present tell us that marvelous accomplishments are possible. It is as though some great person is saying we can do something because he or she did it, made it possible for anyone who wants to try. If we want to practice some fine art, poetry, for example, there are any number of persons who say to us, "I did it." There is Emily Dickinson who had a difficult time with life, was shy and reclusive, and yet wrote beautiful verses which we enjoy now more than ever. If we feel an inclination toward painting, there is Vincent Van Gogh whose background was ordinary, who was poor and struggled. What he did can never be forgotten. If we want to sing, there is Al Jolson or Ella Fitzgerald. If we are musical, there is Beethoven or Glen Miller. If we need athletic examples, there is Jim Thorpe or Babe Ruth.

Heroes not only come out of the past to say that we can do what they did. They are living, real, a part of the world in which we live. Their stories touch us because they are like us. They might seem to have more than we do, to be more intelligent, more graceful, or more gifted. But in reality, when we meet them or read about them, they are remarkably human, had the same kinds of problems and obstacles in their lives that we do. They tell us that almost anything is possible if we can get in the right frame of mind and have determination. We never stop needing heroes.

It sometimes happens that our heroes become unreal, lose their human touch, and move into places we cannot enter. Something takes place which makes them different, as though they were beyond mere humanity and had achieved some special qualities which put them out of reach. Exactly what happens is interesting. Our need for models is so intense we often make them something they aren't at all, dress them in miraculous qualities, make them almost divine. We identify with such heroes perhaps because they have done what we cannot do, have done it for us, and so we need not try. They offer us a dream which cannot come true, a pleasant speculation that life cannot be better because heroism is given to only a few. Not too much can be expected from the rest of us.

We give our reverence to the people who live life fully for us; to the movie star who does what we cannot do, lives richly, knows all the right people, and is always sure and confident about everything; to the athlete who quarterbacks for us, or plays center, or pitches over twenty victories in a single season. We all have our special people: singers, artists, athletes, even the leisured people who live gracefully and accomplish little. It is said with some truth that we need royalty more than royal persons need it.

The church has long recognized this deep need that people have for heroes. From long ago, men and women who led exemplary Christian lives have been proposed to us as models for our own lives. What they accomplished, their dedication and service in imitating the life of Jesus has been recommended to us. If St. Francis of Assisi came from a wealthy family, had every opportunity for power and success, and yet gave it all up to serve God, so can we. If Catherine of Siena had the courage to stand up to authority, even to popes, and accomplished countless good works, so can we who come after.

Again, the notion that we can do what saints did is believable because they were normal human beings like ourselves. If they were not human, if they had some special gifts not given to everybody, the saints, like other heroes, would lose their appeal. Then we could only look at them, admire their deeds, but not even think of imitating them. They would become like works of art to be placed in museums and admired, but not for daily and ordinary use.

Just as people have become over enthusiastic about other heroes, we Christians have done much the same with saints, perhaps more so. In recounting the lives of the saints, there has been a tendency to mix legend with fact. The motivation for this has not been to deceive, but to give the saints their due and to make them fitting models for us who come after them. But misplaced zeal has too often carried us away. The result has been less productive than we would have desired. A saint might be described as having a special calling to sanctity from birth, with hardly any choice on their own part. Feats which defy belief get attributed to the saint from infancy. Saints are often described as having done everything better. They prayed more as children, were more pious as youths. And from early on they had visions and special contacts with God. They managed to avoid the normal attractions in life which pose so much difficulty for the rest of us. Their love of penance and physical hardship goes beyond our lesser abilities. In the end, we are left with the conviction that we could never do what they did. We can love them, admire their deeds, but we could never do it ourselves. We have never experienced this call and, perhaps secretly, hope we never will.

With such a background, most of us have a different notion of who saints are and how we relate to them. We offer some willingness to imitate them, but deep down we know that such models are not for us. As an alternative to imitation, we give praise and honor, a kind of holy congratulations for all they have done. The tradition of the church helps us do this by proposing "saints days" which honor different saints on different days throughout the year. On those days we "remember" what they did, how holy they were, and we ask for their help in our own efforts at holiness.

We honor saints in other ways, too, which add to our

admiration of them. We name our children after them to express our hope that they will be saints in their own way. We honor their "pictures" on holy cards, wall hangings, and statues which remind us of them and make their presence felt in our daily lives. Many people light candles to show reverence and devotion, hoping the saints will pray for them and remember them to God.

It would be foolish to maintain that the stories of the saints have had no real meaning in the church. Saints have often inspired Christians to lives of personal holiness and service. Obviously the saints were good people and accomplished remarkable deeds in their lives. No commentary on the saints should claim that they have no meaning, but rather how our approach might be improved, how we might personally benefit more from their inspiration. It could be that if the saints became more genuine for us, more flesh and blood people like we are, they could serve a better purpose in our lives.

If what we have said so far in this chapter is true of the saints, it is even more true of Mary. If we have tended to surround the lives of the saints with legends and myths about their holiness and extraordinary lives, we have gone even further with the mother of Jesus. Most Catholics have a childhood image of Mary which stays with them throughout their lives. She is pictured as someone who was so perfect in every way that she wasn't like us at all. We can easily imagine Mary praying for hours as a child, completely dedicated to spiritual matters, always thinking about God. We find it difficult to imagine that Mary played with the children down the block, shouted and ran frantically in some game or other. We don't think of her as "normal," with the normal problems which everyone has.

We might not admit it, or maybe we haven't thought of it, but it is easy for us to believe that Mary expected everything which happened to her. We might believe that she wasn't surprised at anything because she had some "inside" knowledge not available to the rest of us. We easily forget that Mary was troubled about her life, confused by Jesus, anxious for him, and sad when she didn't understand, pondering many things in her heart. Obviously, she was extremely sorrowful when he was crucified. She could not have understood.

Catholics deal far less with these realities than with reverence or a sort of semi-worship of Mary. We use titles and reverent expressions toward her. But this has come to mean that we don't have too much in common with her. When we say that Mary was immaculately conceived, or assumed into heaven, or that she is the mediatrix of all graces, those titles make little demand on us. Granted, they give us an opportunity to admire her, but they don't ask what we will do in our own lives to be like her. We were not immaculately conceived nor assumed into heaven. What we are looking for is a model who will assure us that we can do in our lives what she has done in her own.

We have recently begun to ask ourselves whether our approach to the saints and Mary ought to be revised. The key notion in this whole consideration can be expressed in a single question. How much do we have in common with the saints? If it is little, then they are far less inspirational for us than we might have thought them to be. If they were like us, with the same kinds of problems and triumphs, the same kinds of victories and failures, then there is hope. If the saints and Mary had to struggle with life, submit to its ordinary demands, and stay with it the way we all have to do, then their lives could say much to us. They could give us a clear message that accepting the Christian way of life can be a source of satisfaction and accomplishment, something we'd like to do ourselves.

This means we should be able to sort out what was important in saints' lives. For some reason we seem to have concentrated on what might be considered abnormal in the saints, talking about behavior which was even bizarre in their lives. We like to recall that one of the saints threw himself naked into a thorn bush when he had a bad thought. We can remember catechism lessons on saints who beat themselves regularly, wore rocks in their shoes, or lived on top of a pillar all their adult lives. We relish the story of a saint who chased a woman from his room with a hot poker. There are stories of saints who never ate, one who never bathed, some who never sang or laughed. We might have come to equate Christianity with these actions rather than with living life normally in the presence of God, doing good works after the example of Jesus. It is certain that the saints themselves would not describe sanctity in such narrow terms as self punishment or the condemnation of life as a curse. It is very possible that if some of the saints were living today, they might do it differently, still be saints, but approach it some other way. They might be more sensitive, nicer to their communities, and try to be a little less demanding of others.

So the effort for each of us should be to get more comfortable with the saints as ordinary human beings, like ourselves. It is important to understand that they did many of the same things we do. Let us take Mary as an example. She was undoubtedly a normal person with a normal childhood. Her appearance was most likely similar to other Jewish women of her time, dark complexioned with normal Jewish features. It is unrealistic to imagine that Mary was more beautiful than other women of her time, more graceful, cultured, or extremely refined. She might have been. We have no way of telling. It seems more logical that she was not. It would have been more normal. Ordinary people in those days did not strive for beautiful appearance.

The custom in Mary's time was to marry whomever was chosen by one's parents. It is in this way that she came to know and consented to marry Joseph, a tradesman from her town. If divine providence was at work in all this, it is reasonable to assume that Joseph and Mary were not consciously aware of it. They were simply observing the customs of their own day. Anyone can relate to the fact that Mary and Joseph experienced the same reaction as others with regard to their marriage. They hoped for happiness, wanted to find meaning in life, and felt the same anxieties other young people do. To deny them any of these reactions is to place them beyond our own human experience. If saints weren't like we are, we can only observe and admire them but not relate to them as persons who shared our human life.

In a sense it seems more reverent to think of Mary as doing the same things we do. She undoubtedly washed dishes, kept house, visited with the neighbors, prepared meals, and she might even have wished that her life could have been different. People undoubtedly liked her. Jesus asked her to live with John the apostle, and John agreed to take her into his home.

Even though we know little about Mary, or the other saints for that matter, we can assume that their lives had to be similar to ours. There was nothing incredible about them. What is miraculous comes from their ability to take what was quite ordinary and accomplish so much.

Mary deserves to be recognized because she was the mother of Jesus. All the saints deserve recognition because they did something extraordinary, had a special sensitivity to the sick, were dedicated teachers, encouraged groups of people to serve others in some noble way, gave away their possessions, and led simple lives. Every saint testifies that we could do the same things if we chose to.

Our traditional response to the saints has been that of devotion. This means that we remember what the saints did and praise them for their good works. That sort of reaction might be positively criticized with the hope of developing a better understanding of what the saints mean to us. We must realize that the saints do not need our devotion in order to survive. We needn't feel an obligation to have statues and pictures of them to win their favor and approval. Devotion to the saints should rather mean that we are willing in some way to do what they did. To "pray" to a saint, make a novena, for example, should mean that we know something about that saint and are willing to put into practice some of the qualities in his or her life. Up to now we have not done this very well and have contented ourselves rather with praise, singing, saying special prayers, lighting candles, and remembering the saint on his or her feast day.

To praise a saint should mean we are willing to be like that person. If we admire the sanctity of St. Francis of Assisi, we should practice something of his simplicity and poverty. If we want to praise St. Catherine of Siena, we might be more courageous in standing up and defending what we believe. What better way to praise saints? It is our way of saying that what we see in them is worth doing in our own lives.

The saint of saints, whom we have come to call the Queen of Saints, is Mary the mother of Jesus. The very fact of her motherhood commands our attention. But we must not get lost in speculation about what that means. It is easy to miss the fact that there is similar potential in each of us to give birth to Jesus in our own times and circumstances. If Mary accepted the invitation to be God's servant, so must we. We serve God by serving others. We make Jesus live when we do what he did. This, of course, was the motivation of each of the saints. Mary said that God had accomplished great things in her. This was her admission that the human person is capable of wonderful deeds, quite beyond our ability to comprehend. We remember Mary because we believe we can do the things she did. We do not admire her because she did something for us, as if we didn't have to do it ourselves. Her life asks us to do what she did. All of this has far less to do with titles and doctrines than with perceiving who Mary was and how her life is very much like our own.

Whenever a person does something good and meaningful, or contributes something to life, it should be recognized. We try to do this, and we do it best with children because we know they need recognition for their own self-confidence. We don't do quite so well with each other, and often we find it hard to compliment and encourage one another. Who knows why this happens? Maybe we don't want to recognize the good in others because the same quality may be lacking in ourselves. Maybe it is because we get embarrassed when others compliment us. Whatever the explanation, we would do better to recognize that we are a community of people. If someone accomplishes something, everyone benefits. In a sense, we are accomplishing together. If someone in our family, say a brother or sister, does well, wins a contest, writes a book, or graduates with honors, we all feel proud and a part of the victory. When we begin to recognize that we are all members of a larger family, we will be able to take more satisfaction in the accomplishments of others. When that day comes, and for some it is already here, we will recognize more "saints" in our midst and be able to congratulate them more sincerely, and even be "devoted" to them. But at least a part of our devotion will imply that we want to do good things also, be in the mainstream, and never expect them to do our work for us. Rather than light a candle or have a holy card printed for others, we will be occupied with our part in cooperation with all that the human family is striving to do. We will remember those who went before us because of what they did, and we will remember their message that we can do those things also.

We have usually thought of saints as living long ago in circumstances which have no similarity to our own. This tendency has helped to obscure the presence of saints in our own times, contemporary people who share life with us right now. It is easier to think that the age of saints is over. But more to the point, we should begin paying attention to those people who are accomplishing good, exemplifying the gospel message, and demonstrating that it can be done in modern settings. As a matter of fact, there are many modern saints. To attempt a list would be unrealistic, but we immediately think of people who are obviously good and dedicated to the message which Jesus left. These people range from public figures to the lady next door. It is not at all unthinkable that there is sanctity in us; it is quite probable that in some sense we ourselves are saints. We may never be officially recognized, but we share something of the character of those who went before us. If St. Francis became poor by giving up the opportunities available to him in his father's business, we can choose not to make material wealth the first priority in our lives. If Catherine of Siena spoke out against unjust authority, even in popes, we should be willing to speak out also, which might require the same kind of courage.

Some good Christian people lament the fact that we have lost the old reverence we used to have for Mary and the saints. They feel that things were better when we prayed to the saints, had novenas, used more statues, and kept up a sense of communion with them. No one has intentionally stopped these older practices. It is simply that they have gradually diminished and have been replaced by something more realistic.

Perhaps our devotion is stronger than before and we have failed to recognize it. If we believe in the ability of every human person to accomplish good things, we have come a long way. If we accept what Jesus said about our ability to do great things, we can begin to believe in ourselves and begin to believe that God has called us to the fullest possible life. When we stop thinking that saints are few and very special people, we will be moving in a positive direction.

After thinking about it, we might agree that Mary said it best. She told her cousin Elizabeth that God had done great things in her. The very same greatness could happen in each of us. It is a matter of choice.

The high school student might not know who St. Francis or St. Catherine was. This lack of knowledge is a shame, a neglect of our heritage. We should make an effort to remedy that kind of ignorance. But even more important, we should be able to recognize good where we see it, both past and present. God is always doing good, and at least a part of the Christian life is being able to recognize and appreciate it.

Chapter 14

Ecumenism

Just recently at a writers' workshop, I saw an example of ecumenism at work. The conference took place over a weekend, and on Saturday evening the question of Sunday worship came up. Our moderator asked if one of the priests would please offer Mass for those who wished to attend. Turning her attention to those present who were not Catholic, she asked a Methodist minister if he would offer a worship service for their convenience. The minister's response was mildly surprising. He said he'd prefer to attend the Mass and suggested that all who wanted to could do the same; no sense multiplying services when one would do. A short ten or fifteen years ago this would have been more than surprising. It would have shocked us all, and it's quite possible that we would have been offended by such a bold presumption.

The story doesn't end there, however. While we were gathered at Mass, I must admit that I watched the minister with some fascination. When we passed the bread and the cup, he shared it with the rest of us. It seemed quite natural and not at all out of place.

That little episode is in marked contrast to other events regarding religious differences which most of us have experienced. Consider another example. A Catholic woman I know recently told me an experience she had in the 1950s concerning the marriage of her best friend. She had been asked to sing at the wedding and readily accepted the invitation. She didn't think at all about the fact that the wedding was to take place in a Protestant church. Her mother cautioned that she should ask the priest if she could attend the wedding.

Considering the request a mere formality, she mentioned it to the priest the following Sunday after Mass. He replied with finality that she could not attend. She protested mildly, but the priest remained firm. She was ordered not to attend the wedding.

When the young woman told this to her mother, it was with more anger and with the threat that she wouldn't go back to church at all if the priest persisted in being so rigid. After all, this was her best friend. It wasn't as though she were changing religions or would be influenced by the doctrines taught there. She just wanted to do her friend a favor.

With some embarrassment the mother went to speak with the priest. After she explained the situation and pointed out the threat and the disappointment involved, the priest reluctantly consented, but only under the condition that the daughter would in no way participate, only sing, and take no payment for her services.

These days it is common practice for ministers of different denominations to perform ceremonies together, exchange pulpits, share liturgies, pray in common, and much more. Catholics are permitted to marry non-Catholics in a church of another faith, even without the presence of a priest, when it might cause strain or discomfort not to do so.

To say we have come a long way is at least an understatement. In fact, the differences between today's practice and that of former times could not have been predicted just a few decades ago.

Ecumenism is a word used to signify that we are crossing over from a narrower to a much wider view of what religion and worship can be. It is a word we have used for many years in various contexts. The notion of better understanding and mutual acceptance among churches used to be expressed in the hope we all had for church unity. We used to set aside a week of prayer for that. That was a time when we might discreetly visit another church, pray with the people there, and foster a feeling of warmth and even a sense of apology for our mutual estrangement.

It is true that for Catholics church unity or ecumenism signified a secret hope that Protestants would cross over to our way of thinking and accept our truer doctrines. Because our heritage was older and because we knew we were the "true church," we felt that such hopes were reasonable.

How did we arrive at such a situation in which there seemed to be competition and even enmity among religions? At times there was open hatred and rejection of one religion by another. Sometimes ministers used the pulpit to disparage other religions, expressing notions of diabolical forces and the need to avoid any contact with the members of certain churches. Terrible things have been said against religions and religious people. Violent encounters have taken place, as if God intended us to physically suppress the efforts of those who differ from us in religious belief. Sadly, even to this day, wars and killings have taken place in the name of religious faith. It is impossible to believe that God intends such foolishness to come from our so-called religious inclinations.

Perhaps a partial explanation of this embarrassing conduct lies in the defensive posture which has generally been assumed by religions and religious people. Many people have suffered cruel persecution for the religion they professed. Early Christians were imprisoned and even killed for their beliefs. Entire countries pitted themselves against each other because of religious differences. Many wars have been fought over different religious ideologies.

If a given religion became well established and achieved some measure of political acceptability, a jealous defensive stance was taken against any encroachment on it. There was no room for questioning even by those within the church. Evidence of this defensive attitude can be seen throughout history. In the very early days those who voiced dissent or asked for clarification were viewed as heretics. There was very little toleration of such people. Often they were told to recant or suffer dire consequences. We can look back with shame on periods of violent punishment heaped on many well-meaning and sincere people. The Inquisition was a time in the history of the Catholic church which we would very much like to forget. We know that we would never tolerate such meanness again. But attitudes are difficult to change, and a residue of resentment toward those who differ from us lurks somewhere in the darker corners of our being.

When we look back now to the Protestant Reformation and the treatment given other religions and religious people, we have to admit that there was a very real need for change and reformation. When we recall how many people were baptized at the point of the sword, or forced to accept religious belief, we should want to be more tolerant. When we remember that popes were involved in temporal rule, like kings and lords, and sometimes furthered their secular interests in the name of religion, we feel a need to apologize for these abuses.

With that kind of historical background, we can better understand how religious sects and churches have come into modern times colored by attitudes of suspicion and mistrust. Cautious distance is the natural outgrowth of long-standing resentment and hostility. In many cases churches have struggled to maintain themselves while defending against others who threatened their very existence.

Slowly but surely, however, the realization surfaced that religious sects cannot bear such hostility toward one another. An attitude of tolerance began to develop. Talk of unity and mutual contribution became more frequent. And the stage was set for something more.

With the Second Vatican Council, tentative beginnings received strong reinforcement. The council documents on religious tolerance and ecumenism opened the door to broad mutual acceptance among all religions. The documents clearly acknowledged that we have much to learn from others. It was affirmed that we have nothing to fear from other religions. What we had thought of as threatening and injurious to our faith must be relinquished in favor of a saner admission that people who profess religion are sincere and well-meaning. Notions about church unity and ecumenism were clarified. We were asked to replace our old attitudes with new ones. We used to think ecumenism simply meant "we'll tolerate you if you'll tolerate us. We'll accept your religion if you'll accept ours." Such passive ecumenism is more like detente or a holy standoff; it admits very little opportunity for growth. The council intends to ask for much more in keeping with the mind of Jesus. We are being asked to learn from one another. Every religion has something to give to its people and to other religions. Every religion is accomplishing good by caring for its membership.

The spirit of Jesus must be at the heart of ecumenism. Jesus met and accepted all sincere people. He didn't refuse to minister to Roman centurions, a Phoenician woman, Pharisees who came to see him in the night, those who had no particular faith but were seeking. Jesus never asked for conversion to a set of doctrines. He only asked for faith. He often said: "Can you believe?" and granted his ministry freely on the basis of that. He repeatedly got angry with those who equated religious spirit with laws and rituals. He declared that it's what is in the heart that counts.

Ecumenism, then, is much more than an agreement of mutual indifference: "We won't bother you if you don't bother us." It is rather based on the premise that we are always growing and learning in religious faith, and we must be willing to enhance our growth by association with other believers. Ecumenism must become positive and active in seeking to receive what is good in other beliefs and religions. We cannot afford to delude ourselves that we have everything we need.

Every religion seeks to know God and looks for ways to express that quest in meaningful relationships with others who are gathered for the same purpose. Religious people want to experience satisfying contact with what is beyond us, mysterious, transcendent, stretching our imagination and understanding. No religion completely accomplishes all this. But all religions have some degree of meaning and purpose. Obviously, unity in religious expression offers more strength than separatism does. The object of ecumenism is to give and graciously receive what is good from one another. Can what is good ever be undesirable?

All persons sense within themselves longings for fulfillment and peace, security, justice, decency, and so much more. It is natural to want to know God. Hundreds of millions of people want to hear what Jesus said to us and to want to follow the way of life which he proposed for our good. For those who have not heard of Jesus, there is still a deep religious inclination in them to search out the meaning of their lives. Each of us wants to develop the human potential within us. We long to share what is good, giving and receiving in generosity and faith.

Problems and crises of various kinds often upset our security and sense of balance. We are constantly searching out new resolutions for what disturbs our equilibrium and comfort. New and changing demands are always coming into our lives. How do we deal with technology, respect for life, multi-national corporations, corporate justice, exploitation of the weak, third world oppression, and the pervasive sense of negativism toward life? Who helps us deal with the problems of today's youth, the drug culture, a gnawing sense of meaninglessness in life, boredom, inner rage, violence done to the innocent, the warped values of materialism, selfishness, prejudice and rejection?

To think that any one group or religion could solve these and many other problems is totally unrealistic. The spirit of the Second Vatican Council suggests that only through cooperation can we begin to break through much of what has remained impenetrable until now. It is beyond time for seeking help from other groups. Religious denominations would do well to depend on one another in a sense of appreciation for what each possesses and offers from the richness they have acquired through growth and study. Many religions, Catholic and Protestant alike, have been arrogant in the past, pretending they didn't need any help or cooperation from others. Fortunately, these smug attitudes have almost disappeared.

What can we offer one another? From Eastern religions we can learn much about prayer and contemplation which seem to have become obscured in the Western world. We can ask them to teach us something of the sanctity of life, not only of human persons, but of the entire world and every object in it. We often disregard the deep sense of unity which Eastern people maintain with the world and everything in it.

Catholics can benefit tremendously from the extraordinary sense of reverence which most Protestants have for the Word of God. We have perhaps been too confident that God's Word was meant especially for us and that there was no need for personal study of revelation.

Protestants have also reminded us that there is much work to be done in the world. We may be lulled into a sense of complacency arising from our conviction that receiving the sacraments and attending church is enough. The example of many Protestants in service and concern for others should motivate us to strengthen our efforts and reassert our energies toward those in need.

The Catholic church has a rich tradition of ceremony and ritual which gives meaning to worship. Its theology, too, is the result of long study through difficult times.

The notion of ecumenism indicates that we can learn and grow not only from what other religions are saying to us but also from other cultures and philosophies. The American Indian could have taught us much if we had been willing to listen: respect for the land, how to share with others. Philosophers could enrich our lives even though they do not share our religious faith. Sometimes we have dismissed the truth because it was expressed by those who did not believe, or believed differently from us, or even because they belonged to a different political party, were communists or democrats or atheists.

The point is that ecumenism should engender in us a sense of trust of others, a willingness to ask others to assist us. This does not mean that we have no principles to live by or must give up our convictions. It means, not so simply, that we must be an open and growing people, willing to risk something of ourselves in order to progress.

There are some who say that the Second Vatican Council's decrees on ecumenism and religious tolerance were short lived in their effects. True, there were some efforts in the beginning, but what started with promise waned into tokenism. Some say that we are back to where we were before it all began. Maybe there was some progress, but we have not come to any significant juncture where we could say that great strides have been made.

Perhaps that is true to a certain extent, but in the end it calls for qualification. One cannot deny that much has changed and much is in progress among those in the pews. The document on ecumenism has accomplished its work in local churches and in certain congregations. There is a sense of fellowship and acceptance among people of different religious denominations which did not exist just a few years ago.

Ecumenism is a reality in the lives of many people. In a number of places there are study groups composed of persons of different religions. These have been able to replace the old feelings of competition and distance with warmth and confidence that good things can come from dialogue. In some instances ministers of various faiths are meeting for mutual assistance and sharing concerning the problems in their individual parishes. The big difference in these meetings is the new sense of trust and respect which the ministers have for one another. A notable feature is the participation of Catholic priests at these gatherings. While it is true that Protestant ministers participated regularly in such meetings in the past, priests generally absented themselves out of a sense of self-sufficiency. This attitude has changed in the lives of most priests.

In many ways, there has been much more cooperation in attacking the many problems of our time: hunger, marital difficulties, child abuse, housing, social injustice, and many more. It is common today for various congregations to share facilities, pool resources, volunteer labor for special needs, and participate in parish picnics. These are healthy signs of growth, and they witness to the fact that much is being accomplished.

Many causes go beyond individual parishes. A rally to protest the use of nuclear weapons can be an occasion for meeting people of all different faiths and even no faith at all. To discuss the plight of migrant workers, those on welfare, single parents, or the sorrows of the divorced, calls for something beyond the limits of one's own faith. Very few people today would refuse to contribute to the solution of social problems on the basis of religious differences.

If ecumenical cooperation and respect are still not what they should be, they are better than they were before. The positive aspect is that each of us has a choice.

We can choose to move in directions which require much more from each of us. We can remain silent, "obedient" to our passive religious convictions. Or we can speak out our belief in the exhortation of Jesus to preach the good news to others by our presence and our participation in their concerns. We may remain uninvolved, living in isolation or only with those who think as we do. Or we can risk the possibility of growth and proceed into greater involvement. We can spend our energies over points of personal morality, legalism about how our church is right and others are wrong. Or we can be filled with a spirit of close relationship to every living person, feeling ourselves a part of that life which involves us all. It is our choice. It is a choice to be ecumenical.

If the minister at that writers' conference had an effect on us, it should have been positive. We should have been thankful that something of that consequence could happen in our time. This was far better than what went before. What happened at that worship service replaced mistrust, suspicion, and a sense of resentment. It was very good. It was a step toward what might be. We are a family in God and brothers and sisters to all with whom we experience the gift of life.

Chapter 15

What is the layperson's role in the church?

Ministry is defined as the active assistance we offer to others in helping to meet their needs. We minister when we listen attentively to someone who is depressed, when we help someone get a job, take a casserole to the family who is grieving over the death of one of their members, assist the poor people in the community who need clothes and food. We minister when we share our experiences with others, saying that we sympathize, understand, and are willing to participate in their needs. The deepest meaning of ministry comes from our willingness to help one another see something spiritual, holy, and meaningful in life, no matter how bad or good it might be at the present moment. The opportunity for ministry comes at every moment by the very fact of our presence to one another. No life exists without need. No person can ever say that he or she can live without reliance on others.

Ministry never implies that we are better than those to whom we minister. The whole purpose of helping others is to bring them to a level equal to our own. To minister to others with the conviction that they are less and we are greater, however, completely misses what Jesus had to say about service and ministry. He told us that we must be last, the least in the kingdom and like slaves we cannot be greater than our master; and our master was willing to wash other people's feet.

The history of ministry in the Catholic church has not always accurately reflected this attitude of Jesus. We have been inclined to place those in official ministry, those in the clerical state, in a special position in the church which is based on superiority, deeper holiness, closeness to God, more learning in divine matters, and special divine selection. Popes, bishops, priests, and sisters have often been regarded as the only true ministers, those specially designated to be the genuine representatives of God's will for the people.

The early church had a different notion of ministry. From the beginning there was a sense of the different contributions which could be made by all the different members. Luke, in the Acts of the Apostles, offers a description of the mutual sharing practiced by all those who sought membership in the community. One might serve at table, another might preach the word, someone else cared for the elderly. Additionally, St. Paul wrote to the Corinthians, reminding them that the community possessed a variety of gifts because of the variety of the members. He said one might have the gift of prophecy, another the gift of healing, a third the gift of preaching, and still a fourth the gift of speaking in tongues, and so on. It was by using these various gifts that the community functioned. In a later chapter, Paul ends the whole consideration by reminding everyone that all of these gifts must be bound together and infused with the greatest of gifts, love.

Somewhere in the history of the church, for reasons which are difficult to understand, Christians began to mistrust the fact that they had any gifts at all in the area of ministry. They began to leave the responsibility of service to particular persons who signified by express intention that they were interested in accepting the office of ministry. We began to think of ministry as requiring training and a special vocation not open to everyone. Perhaps more by permission than by intention, we expected less and less of everyone other than clerics, priests and sisters, and accepted the fact of their superior position. Such a condition has prevailed up until just recently, and we are now beginning to realize that we have inadvertently neglected the invitation which every Christian has to minister to the needs of others. We had expected too little of ourselves and became unaware, in ecclesiastical thinking at least, of the gifts which God has given to all of us.

Since the Second Vatican Council, however, we have come into what many like to call "the age of the layperson." This means that we must begin to look to one another to fulfil the needs which each of us has in our lives. The decree of the Vatican Council on the role of the layperson is an expression of confidence that every person has much to offer. The church will actually be nowhere near fulfilling the expectations which God has for each of us until we become much more aware of the need which every member of the Christian community has to minister. We are called to help one another and to accept the opportunity of living out the command of Jesus that we be personally responsible for our sisters and brothers. It is a time of challenge, a call to everyone to begin with new enthusiasm, to recognize that the kingdom only becomes visible through the efforts of every Christian person.

Because of all this, we have seen momentous changes in the last twenty years. Those who study these matters feel that what we have seen is only a beginning, and there is much more to come. In contrast to former times when priests or sisters were considered to be pretty much the only official ministers in the church, many laypersons today are coming forward and assuming positions of ministry which they never held before. They are beginning to teach and instruct, formally in classrooms and informally in homes, among families and interested groups. It is not at all unusual for laypersons to hold high degrees in theology, to enroll at colleges and universities in programs leading to master and doctoral degrees in Scripture or in moral or dogmatic theology. Whereas spiritual counseling was almost exclusively the role of the priest in the past, many professional counselors today see their service as a significant aspect of ministry. These people are able to look upon their work as a vocation which is comparable to that of the priest or sister.

A wide variety of ministerial service is open to the layperson in almost every parish. Parishioners are being asked to come forward, make themselves known, and to accept new roles offered to them. At a Sunday Mass one is likely to see laypersons distributing communion, reading the Scriptures, participating actively in the liturgy by singing, responding to the celebrant, and much more. The liturgy might very well have been prepared by a committee of laypersons. Those present might be called upon to discuss the theme of the Mass, make the announcements, and even offer some thoughts on subjects having to do with social action, care of those in need in the parish, or campaigning for parish offices.

Parish councils have appeared in recent years. They offer a sincere invitation to people to take their places in the administration and decision-making processes which should be a part of every Christian community. There is a new spirit in many people, a willingness to share responsibility. This development does not rest easily with some pastors who for years determined everything, making unilateral decisions about building, remodeling, and spending; they may even have swept the church steps and counted the Sunday collection. But these things are changing in our age of accountability and window opening.

The age of lay ministry has been accelerated by many things, not the least of which is the growing shortage of clergy around the world. In the United States, for example, there are many parishes which have only one priest in residence where before they might have had two or three. This situation has made pastors more dependent on the members of the congregation. The same holds true for sisters, who once almost exclusively taught in schools, managed religious education programs, assisted in preparation of liturgy, and even helped with the administration of the parish. Many see the shortage of clergy as a mixed blessing; it calls forth from the layperson gifts and talents in ministry which might otherwise have been left unused. They maintain that the end result will be a healthier church, restoring to its members a welcome sense of belonging and contribution. There are others who say that even if there weren't a shortage in vocations, the layperson would still insist on his or her proper place in ministry, simply based on the fact that this is a changing world which demands more perceptive appreciation of what people have to give.

Many theologians, bishops, and others have claimed that the ideal of ministry is fulfilled when people are called forth by the community itself. The members of a particular parish are in the best position to see the needs which exist within that community. They can also tell which members of the community will work out best in fulfilling those needs. The call of the community itself to certain members constitutes the best kind of vocation. The members then "empower" that person or persons to act with the community in pursuing the desired objectives. It is as though the community is saying to a person: "We know that you are a good teacher, or can identify with the thinking of young people, or have a love for good liturgy. We are asking you to accept our request to be a teacher, a youth director, a distributor of communion."

The healthier the community, the more each member will be asked to take his or her place in the total structure. It is not entirely unthinkable that sometime in the future, communities will ask certain individuals to assume offices which were traditionally reserved to priests.

Whenever ministry is discussed in our times, the

subject of women comes up and the position of the official church with regard to their hope to be admitted to equal roles with men. We recently heard a lot of discussion about whether women should be in ministry and to what extent. Not too long ago the pope issued a carefully researched statement about women's ordination to the priesthood. It was his contention that women were not legitimate subjects for ordination since Jesus himself did not ordain any. There was no scriptural reference which women could point to to prove the contrary. There was also a statement to the effect that if Jesus had wanted women priests, he would have ordained his own mother, an exemplary woman who certainly would have had the necessary holiness and dedication. This statement evoked mixed feelings and expressions. Some welcomed a final and clear statement from the official church. They hoped that in this way the issue would be settled once and for all. There were others who strongly protested the statement, pointing out that little else could be expected from a church in which all the real power rested in the hands of males.

Those who protested maintained that the arguments against women's ordination were weak and ill-founded. To say that Jesus didn't want women priests because he never ordained any is irrelevant. Jesus ordained the apostles, many of whom were married. How can we therefore say that the clergy must not be married? If we respond by saying that the church can change in this regard, why can't it change with regard to the ordination of women? Those who disagree with the statement of the pope further maintain that too much is taken for granted. Is it possible that this whole issue wasn't even a concern for Jesus? Was he living in a culture which would not have accepted women priests? Has culture changed to accept the presence of women in ministry since that time? Didn't Jesus associate with women, an unprecedented behavior for that time in history? Didn't he address issues of real importance, something which no one ever did? What was it he meant to say by this type of action?

Whatever the final outcome of this struggle, we should make some observations about the position of women in ministry. First, we should admit that the traditional stance of the church toward women was no different from that of the larger society, one of oppression and abuse. If anything, the lot of women in the church was worse than in the world. There is much evidence which shows that to be female was to be inferior. This fact was universally accepted and virtually unquestioned.

Testimony that women were considered inferior in the church can be seen in the consistent use of male-oriented language. The male pronouns, he and him, abound in liturgical language and theology texts. Our prayers have asked that God save "mankind," "all men," declaring that Jesus came for the sake of "man." We generally respond by maintaining that these are general terms which include both men and women. But such responses miss the point of why we distinguish men from women in the first place. Although many more women attended church than men, they were prohibited from equal participation in liturgy and ceremony. No women could enter the sanctuary without explicit permission. Certainly no female could serve Mass, something reserved for men who were obviously chosen to fill the more important roles in ministry. Women were made to wear hats in church, indicating their different status before God.

The teaching of the church regarding marriage heavily emphasized the superior position of the male. Wives were expected to be submissive toward their husbands. In the area of sexuality, the husband assumed the dominant role, specifying when and how sexual exchange should occur. It was the wife's lot to be obedient and undemanding. She was counseled never to refuse marital rights unless they were explicitly sinful. Every wife had to "follow" her husband wherever and whenever he decided.

It was not expected that women would make any significant contributions to the study or progress of theology. The assumption always was that theology was the domain of males. Until recently, no academic courses in theology were offered to women. Even nuns had no theological training other than what they could personally acquire or what could be gained from retreats and seminars. Women in religion were primarily teachers who were to communicate the teaching of the official church. Beyond that role, they were to prepare children for the sacraments, assist the pastor in his work, and perhaps take care of the sick and elderly.

Mysteriously, in spite of the unequal treatment which women have received at the hands of the church, many more of them are involved in church ministry and church attendance than men. Any priest who has any pastoral experience will readily admit that women in ministry are dependable, willing and effective. Some have said this is because women have more leisure time and less responsibility. But we are beginning to suspect that generally men have less interest in religion than women do.

The debate about the role of women in the church is far from over. The whole issue about women in ministry has called for extensive changes and the recognition that women have much to offer. What has happened in the church is reinforced by what is happening to women generally at every level of society. To ignore these issues would be foolish, deluding ourselves that these concerns will peacefully go away.

So for the first time in the history of the church we are beginning to officially acknowledge the presence and talent of women. This admission opens the way to further admissions that women are equal to men in sensitivity toward service, sympathy and compassion, organization and decision making.

The interest of women in religion can further be seen from their involvement at the parish level. Parish projects from organizing picnics to major undertakings are supported to a large extent by women. Liturgy committees, social action groups, religious education programs, discussion and study efforts, to name only a few, always have more women involved than men. On Sunday mornings one can easily see who sings, responds, participates, and prays aloud. There is a kind of unwritten rule among men that participation in religion is a sign of weakness, something that only women do. All this is a continuing source of amazement when we consider that women have every reason not to participate, but rather, because of harsh treatment, to leave the church entirely. Unfortunately, many have.

This is not to say that all men are disinterested, irreligious, and passive. It is simply that women's interest in the affairs of the church is much more apparent than men's. That there are many superb and sensitive men in any parish is undeniable. What is being said today is simply that women, who have been neglected in the past, are generally more willing to continue in service and ministry in the church than men are. Some people believe that these characteristics distinguishing women from men in the practice of religion are cultural and not necessarily a permanent quality of human nature. There have been times of deep devotion and religious dedication on the part of men. There certainly could be a return of much which has become less visible in the church today.

These are some of the realities in today's church. Some see them as bleak and depressing, while others are encouraged by what can develop from these circumstances. Recent forecasts speak about the gradual disappearance of ministry as we know it. One Catholic newspaper recently predicted that the priesthood in its present form will be a thing of the past by the year 2000. If this will be the case, ministry will certainly have to change. Such predictions can be judged as unrealistic, lacking in faith in what Jesus said about being with the church until the end of time. But even if such a radical situation does not come to pass, we can be sure that ministry will change. It has already. What direction it will take is not certain;

but what is certain is that many more people in the ranks of the church will assume much more responsibility than they did in the past.

In some senses there is nothing radically new about this direction in ministry. At various times in the past when for some reason or other ministers were unavailable, individuals and sometimes whole countries have persevered in faith and practice. In Japan, for instance, when priests were absent for hundreds of years, Christians preserved the fundamentals of their religion and continued to practice the faith. Even in the United States, people in remote areas retained their faith long after available ministers left. While today's situation is somewhat different, ministers haven't exactly left the area, there are enough similarities to have confidence that Christians are quite capable of preserving the faith and continuing its practice.

Here is a modern story about people who assumed roles in ministry. Yolanda Lallande began her ministry in Mexico at a leper colony where there was no priest or minister. People there were dying almost every day, others were suffering the pains of leprosy, all were in need of consolation and comfort. When Yolanda asked about the possibility of getting a priest to work among the lepers, she was told that none was available. It was then that she began to go to the leprosarium herself. She baptized many of the children, prayed with those who were dying, even anointed them. She conducted liturgies, very similar to the Mass, but with no words of consecration. Occasionally a priest gave her some consecrated hosts to distribute to the people. Yolanda came to be considered as much a minister as an ordained priest. She continued to minister in the most Christlike sense, moving among the lepers with compassion and sympathy, never complacent or mediocre in her care for them.

The story does not end here, but continues in an even more astounding way. It happened that the priest in her own parish suddenly left without explanation or farewell. Again, there was no priest to take his place. Yolanda gathered with the other members of the parish, and they determined that they would continue to meet and minister to one another. They met on Friday evening to prepare the Sunday liturgy. Each week they offered readings, homilies, prayers, and they distributed communion which had been obtained from the cathedral in the town. From the beginning they informed the bishop of their activities. On one particular Sunday, he attended the liturgy, listened to the homily, and received communion with the people. After the liturgy, the bishop encouraged the people of the parish to continue what they were doing, and he complimented Yolanda and those who assisted her.

Is this the church of the future? Not necessarily. But the story indicates that ministry which is indeed effective can take various forms. Undoubtedly such happenings are taking place in other parts of the world, especially in remote areas.

It is the contention of some people who study ministry that the people in the church are much more ready to assume roles of ministry than officials in the church are willing to admit. There is good evidence that this is true. It is difficult for bishops and priests to accept the fact that a number of people in any congregation could immediately make a significant contribution to the health of the parish, give effective sermons, teach effectively, administer, see to the needs of those in pain, and be understanding and sensitive. But such attitudes are diminishing, and much is being accomplished already.

The message which Jesus left us continues to have its effect in our time. It will continue to be effective long after our time. We have inherited what has gone before, and we must make our own contribution to the growth of the church. Jesus said we should care for one another. He told us that if we believed, we would be able to do what he did and even more. It was his solemn charge that we should be recognized by how we love one another. He often reminded us that we must serve, relieve, support, and sanctify. He assured us that God has called us into the kingdom and accepts us because of Jesus. We believe this because of our faith. To want to make it known to others, declare it to the world for its own good, is ministry. To celebrate that good news by ceremony and ritual is sacramental ministry. This ministry belongs to all of us because we have been asked to participate, to respond to what God has offered to us.

It is conceivable that there are many ways to come into the kingdom. Jesus himself said that there are many mansions in God's house. It is unrealistic to contend that any particular minister or ministry is essential to salvation. It is rather through the ministry of the entire community, the collected talents and gifts of all people, that God becomes fully known to the world. God will be present in our lives and we will still be able to praise and worship, regardless of the direction of ministry. The form and presentation of ministry have changed in the church in the past. It is changing in our own time. It is good that we can trust that change will always be toward progress and growth. The progress is not always immediately apparent, but in the final analysis, it manifests itself.

There will always be ministry. Some will always respond to the needs of others. Where these are, the poor will be attended, the naked clothed, those without homes given shelter. Because Jesus has come to the world and offered the challenge of his life to us, we will continue to preach the gospel, assist those in pain and heal those who are suffering. It might be at times that ministry will not be as effective as at other times. It might also be that ministry will become something living, extremely effective, better than anything which we have known so far in the history of Christianity. But whatever the case, every Christian person is called to offer his or her gift. It is our time to teach, to heal and speak in tongues, to prophesy and proclaim the presence of God among people. It cannot be the task of a few to accomplish this, but rather the challenge offered to every one among us.

Chapter 16

The social message
of the Gospel

There is hardly a page in the gospels where Jesus is not seen helping to relieve the needs and problems of people. He is described as responding immediately to cure the sick servant of the Roman centurion. He is concerned enough to stop everything to heal the paralysis of a man brought to him on a pallet and lowered through the roof. He takes time to talk to strangers, to offer an encouraging word to a tax collector, to forgive an adulteress, to befriend a prostitute, feed a multitude of people, and even to break the law to cure the sick on the Sabbath day. No one is insignificant, nothing too incidental to merit his attention. He is so in tune with his mission to care for the needs of others that the very touch of his garments has power. The overwhelming miracle of his life was not only that he was able to cure, heal, relieve, encourage, and minister, but also that he was so intensely interested, so consistently ready and open to all who approached him.

The consistent exhortation which Jesus urged on his apostles was that they should continue to do in their lives what he had done in his. He said he was sending them as he himself had been sent. He affirmed that service was the most important element in the good news, and he washed the apostles' feet to illustrate the importance of the message. He told them to be last, slaves rather than masters, serving rather than demanding service.

The early Christian community understood what Jesus had said about responding to one another, being concerned to care for those who had less. Members are described as living together, holding all things in common, and caring for the needs of one another. Early writers simply said that no one went without what was necessary, and those who had more shared with those who had less. Many sold their possessions and "laid them at the feet of the apostles," to be used as they judged fit on behalf of the other members of the community.

If Jesus came primarily to help those who were poor and in need, the church will be authentic only to the extent that it continues this specific mission. To the degree that the church relinquishes this priority, it will be less effective in carrying out the intention of Jesus. It is less significant that the church has amassed great treasures in art, buildings, and property, has significant social and political power in the modern world, has gained a large and growing membership through conversion, and is involved in the struggle of world affairs. The single criterion by which we will know that the kingdom of God is among us will always be that those who are in need, the poor, have the good news spoken to them. If the poor go wanting, the church is wanting on the earth.

While these are simple truths, reflecting the simplicity of Jesus, they are not easy to incorporate into our lives. Historically we have been accused of wanting to cover them over, interpret them to mean something less demanding and more comfortable. Some have misconstrued what Jesus was saying and gone so far as to claim that success and wealth in this world are sure signs of God's approval, pointing toward certain eternal reward. We sometimes resent those who are in need, saying that it is their own fault, something for which they could find a remedy if they were willing to try. We have often said these things amidst our wealth and excess in the Christian church. Jesus never once spoke about those who were deserving. It wasn't a priority in his life. When we read the gospels, we get the distinct impression that those in need at that time, like all of us at any time, didn't have any right to what Jesus gave them. They were simply in need.

It is easy to lose sight of Jesus' message that we should be concerned for the least of our brothers and sisters. It is easy to rationalize that there is really little we can do in the way of service and response to one another. While we have not consciously relinquished the mission which Jesus gave us to care for one another's needs, the importance of that mission might have begun to dim in the midst of many other aspects of the Christian life. We have placed greater emphasis on believing in doctrines, following rules, observing commandments, and supporting our parishes.

If we haven't forgotten it, we may at least have set aside the description which Jesus offered John the Baptist's disciples when they asked John's question, "Are you he who is to come or shall we look for another?" Jesus replied, "Go and tell John that the blind see and the dumb speak, the deaf hear and the lame walk. And the poor have the gospel preached to them."

Since the time of Jesus the church has grown to be an imposing and unbelievably wealthy institution. It has acquired vast holdings in land, buildings, artifacts, and beautiful objects which the world esteems. In modern times the church has been referred to as the richest institution in the world. We have rationalized that such material wealth serves two purposes. First of all, it enables the church to fulfill its mission of preaching the gospel to all nations, keeping abreast of the times and the technological advances of the world. Secondly, its riches reflect the church's dignity, the visible kingdom of God on earth. It is only in recent years that we have begun to painfully reexamine the validity of these claims. The conclusions we are reaching demand much more of us than we have admitted in the past. Much which is healthy and promising is coming to light. People at all levels in the church are beginning to seek new directions toward more authentic approaches to the gospel message and the use of the world's goods.

Where the church has responded to the needs of those who look to it for assistance, it has sometimes lost much of its energies in studies, surveys, and analyses. Any institution, and therefore the church, can become overcrowded with committees, bureaus, task forces, study groups, and pilot programs, whose energies are neutralized with too much organizational structure. Sometimes the organization becomes more important than the work it is trying to accomplish. Much attention is paid to how things should be done, and less to what is actually being accomplished.

If we return to the person of Jesus, we find a simplicity which motivates us to reexamine the work of the church and every Christian. St. Peter described Jesus as one who "went about doing good." We find in the gospels that Jesus was most sensitive in his approach to people. He wore no special clothing, had no title of eminence or dignity, even shunned any special recognition or acclaim. It is here that we find the essence of his concern for others, an effort to avoid being different from the people with whom he was in daily contact.

Since the Second Vatican Council we have become more concerned with reflecting that image of Jesus so obvious in the gospels. We are seeing a long-needed shift in emphasis from concern for the image and internal health of the church to the needs of the majority of persons in the world who are hungry, unjustly treated, economically exploited, enslaved to poverty, and often living in despair. This shift is supported and encouraged by Christians at all levels within the church. This shift in emphasis has left very few unaffected by what has happened. It has become increasingly difficult to remain neutral to all that has happened.

Because of this new thinking, we have witnessed some radical changes. We have a fuller awareness of the meaning of the Christian life in concern for others. Sermons in most churches include frequent references to the needs of others, our obligations to our neighbors in other parts of the world who are suffering oppression and want. Today's church speaks plainly about boycotts and involvement in issues of discrimination and unfair wages. We are becoming more aware that we cannot live our lives within the confines of parish boundaries with no consciousness of the many people in the world who look to us for relief and a share of the world's goods. We are beginning to ask questions about what obligations our great wealth implies toward those who have less, who don't even eat well. We can no longer ignore the hunger of two-thirds of the world's population. We are beginning to understand that God cares for us through one another and those who are in need can only know God's care for them through our personal concern to feed and heal, minister and comfort.

This consciousness of the gospel message should begin with those who are dedicated to ministry—bishops and priests, religious men and women. But through their example and service, the whole body of the church should be focused more fully on these interests. The importance of this sensitivity should be taught by example and action. It is impossible to deceive ourselves in these matters. So long as we continue to make other values which have to do with personal comfort, leisure, and wealth a priority in our lives, we are not catching the message of the gospel.

Responding to the social message which Jesus left us must begin with concrete decisions, clearly made and manifested to others, especially those in need. When we become more comfortable with the common people, poor in spirit and circumstance, than we are with the rich and powerful, those in need will begin to look to us with confidence. When we begin to deemphasize our need for wealth and material goods, we will begin to better fulfill the command of Jesus to live for others, to share our surplus, to give away the things we only rarely use or never at all, then we will be able to say confidently that the kingdom of God is among us.

The effects of this kind of thinking are already taking place. We may have only a limited view of what is happening, but the movement is growing in many forms and places.

Many contend that there must be a more equitable distribution of the world's goods. There are those who maintain that the Christian community must become the model of service in these times, using its goods for the benefit of all. A question must be seriously asked. Did God intend there be such a disproportionate distribution of the world's goods, in which many do not even have enough to eat and a few have more than they can possibly ever use? Mary said to Elizabeth that God was indeed great because he championed the lowly, exalted the humble, "has filled the hungry with good things and sent the rich away empty handed."

The church is changing in the area of social responsibility and beginning to ask questions which have not been so boldly asked in the past. Can the wealth of an entire nation, even of the whole world, be controlled by just a few people whose number diminishes every day? Was it meant that the great mass of people in the world should be dependent on almost the whim of a few who have unbelievable power and wealth? These are serious questions, demanding serious answers; and the answers do not always lead to peaceful consent. Sometimes violent struggle accompanies the demands of those who are desperate in their needs.

The theology of liberation, contending that every person in the world has a right to share in the earth's goods, offers hope to those who are seeking even the decencies of life. Liberation theologians maintain that the human spirit can be denied only so long before it rebels, even violently, and demands retribution and compensation for all the ills which it has been made to suffer. Poverty and

destitution have become the subject of high level confer-
ences in the church among bishops and priests. A few
years ago, a conference at Medellin, Columbia, declared
that gross injustices exist in the world. Poor people are
exploited for the profit of a few. Richer nations are mis-
using the poorer ones for the purposes of selfish gain.
This conference recommended that new ways should be
found by which the goods of the earth could be more
equally shared with particular sensitivity to those who
are hungry and in need of housing and health care services.

Pope John Paul's visits to Mexico and South America
emphasize the concern which the church is developing
toward the poorer people of the world. We must begin to
reflect the life of Jesus, whose message was one of compassion toward those who were in need. It is unthinkable
that the members of the Christian church would participate in systems of government whose object is to per-
petuate the continual degradation of the poor for the comfort and good of a few. There is too much evidence that
the Catholic church has not always been completely free
of such questionable involvement. So-called pious Christians have exploited and misused those in positions of
servanthood, tenant farmers, and factory workers, with
too little compensation for them and too little share in
profits.

Many other changes are taking place in the church.
We are offering ministry to all people. We are beginning
to recognize the needs of minority and racial groups. This
begins with apologizing for centuries of neglect and complacency, tokenism and secondary treatment. To minorities we must say that we have been negligent, ignoring
their needs and refusing to see the many problems and
deep wounds which they have suffered for so long. Whatever rejection they might show to our society must be
patiently understood, for so much abuse and indignity
have been heaped upon them in the past. While we may
protest that much of what has happened is not our

personal fault, there is still too much which is—ghettos, lack of opportunity, mediocre education, secondary medical treatment, hasty imprisonment, disproportionate military service, and limited work opportunities. The ministry of Jesus needs to offer so much more to them than has been offered so far; "spiritual encouragement" to accept life the way it is without doing anything to improve it is a sham.

If change in our awareness of the social message of the gospel is to take place, it must begin with recognition. It continues with the efforts of people who are concerned about the needs of those who suffer neglect and lack of care. It is to the credit of the modern church that it has changed its attitude toward the injustices of the past and present. To ignore them would be to miss what is intrinsic to the ministry that Jesus asked of the church and its members.

It is becoming apparent that we have to begin examining the methods we have used in responding to the poor, hungry, and dependent. Because we have always been more or less a part of the state, it has been natural for the church to imitate the state system with regard to welfare and public assistance. The state has placed heavy stress on organization, caring for people by first determining who is qualified, being on guard against those who are unworthy. While there is some validity to this procedure, such an approach can easily become top-heavy and over-organized. There is often too much investigation, bureaucracy, and loss of energy in committees, offices, and details. The welfare world is filled with stories of duplicate and triplicate forms, affidavits and testimonials which amount to overwork with few results.

It has always been to the credit of the Christian churches that there is less detail and demand than in the state structure with regard to public assistance. This is, of course, as it should be. There is still much to be learned from the compassionate attitude of Jesus, who never asked many questions and made very few demands of those he assisted. The basic requirement for any meaningful approach to those in need must, of course, be a spontaneous love of people, a desire for the welfare and good of every person. If we are improving in these areas in the church, this is indeed healthy, of great benefit. If we can change enough to want the same good for others as we do for ourselves, then the kingdom of God will truly have arrived.

There are other areas which are at least indirectly related to the social message of the gospel. One of these has to do with the Catholic church's approach to those who were previously married and those who have chosen to remarry. Jesus came healing, responding to the hurts and pains which the people of his time were experiencing. Can it be any different in our own time? The traditional approach to those whose marriages have ended in divorce has been one of withdrawal. We have denied them the sacraments, refused to recognize their state because of remarriage, and have taken privileges away from them. We have left them with heavy obligations, the demand that they continue to practice their faith, but without its normal compensations. The best we could offer them was our wish for eventual satisfaction through their sacrifice and patient acceptance.

Happily, we have begun to change by offering compassion and understanding. We still have far to go in rectifying so many wrongs toward those who have had difficulty in marriage. We have been unjust in claiming that those whose marriages have held together are more justified than those who, many times through no fault of their own, have not been so fortunate.

Much has been done in recent years to minister to the elderly, shut-ins, and those isolated from the mainstream. We are more aware of our duty and privilege to minister to the sick and dying. Our approach to death is much healthier now, seeing it as a passage into another level of life rather than a punishment. We have begun to respond with more kindness, compassion, and gentleness, putting aside the cold and official stances which were sometimes characteristic of the church in the past.

Good things are happening in individual parishes; people are becoming more aware of the needs which exist outside the confines of their smaller worlds. We are making one another aware that people are suffering in other places and that we can help them. Parishes are awakening to the fact that boycotts and sympathy programs can actually help workers on farms and in factories, improving the lot of those who help to produce the products which we use. Along with these efforts is the growing realization that, whereas we may not be able to change the face of the world overnight, it is still necessary that we do something and share in some way with those who are suffering.

Many parishes give generous tithes of their own income to those who have less, certain projects to help the poor. They support parishes in other countries, respond to local needs, as well as to those within the parish. These tithes take priority over other projects such as enlarging parish plants or building new rectories, or adding on for its own sake.

We must invite the poor, those in need, minorities, the less educated, the simple, and all those marginal people with whom Jesus felt so comfortable into full participation in our parishes. They must serve on parish councils, education boards, and decision-making bodies. They will come, perhaps with skepticism and suspicion, needing our constant assurance that we value their presence and their contribution to the good of the parish. Otherwise we are only a few elite people guarding our own welfare, fearful of the risk of sharing life with others than those we acknowledge as "our own kind."

We must not give the impression that acceptance in the church is conditioned by financial qualifications or personal possessions. We must somehow give genuine welcome to everyone who comes to us, so there is no distinction among persons and no social barriers.

The gospel is a paradox, something we do not readily understand, a message which requires constant inquiry and study. But in one sense it is clear that we are to accept the command of Jesus to live our lives as he did his. He does not ask us to do more than he did. But he does not excuse us from doing less. We tend to judge that what Jesus did was somehow easier for him, since he was specially sent, the Son of God, divine himself. If that were true, the whole message could not apply to us because we would be disqualified by our lack of equality with him. But Jesus was like us, which means that he had all the same inclinations and feelings that we do. All of that makes what he did possible for us also. If any change is needed in our approach to the gospel, it is toward the conviction that we are capable of doing what Jesus did.

Perhaps we will never fully understand much of what Jesus said. It is too full, too rich for a lifetime. But we are called to continue to probe, to consider, and always to make an effort to appropriate what we can. If Jesus said, "Blessed are the poor in spirit," we must continually strive for some kind of real poverty in our lives, something of simplicity, being able to do with less and even without where that is possible. If he further said that we should sell what we have and give it to the poor and follow him, we have to try to understand that, assist the poor in whatever way we can, and be willing to share our lives with others, even to the point of personal sacrifice. If it is harder for a camel to pass through the eye of a needle than for a rich person to be in the kingdom, then we must see that our riches assist us to become poor enough to leave them behind where that is necessary, in the face of the needs of others, in sharing our lives with them. If God sends the rich away empty, then we must not be rich but poor enough to be filled with the truly good things of this world, concern, care, and love for others. If the Christian is described as one who, upon the request for his or her coat, gives away even more, we should be generous enough to clothe those who are naked, not because they deserve it, but because Jesus has assured us that it is a good thing to do. The Christian, according to the commission of Jesus, lends money without hope of return, is last, loses life before ever hoping to find it, serves rather than demands service, and gives freely away.

Was Jesus kidding, winking his eye when he said these things? Was it only for his time, a simpler era in history? These are only glib and irrational claims. There is something eternal and unchangeable about his message, fully applicable in our own time. We have too often missed the message, have thought we were special and had a right to our possessions to the exclusion of others; we have wanted to be better, possess more, exercise our rights, and accept our wealth because God gave it to us as our own, no strings attached.

Jesus said that the kingdom begins small, like mustard seeds. We are beginning, perhaps in small ways, but with the hope that we will grow and flourish. We are beginning to take hold. Many more are becoming concerned and active on behalf of others. Perhaps more now than at any time in history, people are ministering to one another. In remotest places in the world, people are being fed, housed, and clothed. The hands of mercy and tenderness are caressing those who are in need, suffering, and dying. There are sources of support and courage which assist those who have less, who work without just compensation, are in pain for lack of response in their lives. There are those who give their lives for others, freely and without demand.

It is to this that we have been called. To think we have been called to less is to miss the message or to misconstrue the meaning. Our call speaks to a better time, a time of change, in which all things are restored in Jesus, when no one is in need and whatever goods we have are shared in common with those in the community, even the community of the world.

Chapter 17

New directions in the search for God

Religion isn't what it used to be. And neither is anything else for that matter. Gone are the old reliable standbys which were so much a part of our lives in the past. Things have changed. Everything from Saturday afternoon matinees, one western, a mystery, a serial, and two comedies, to the old swimming hole and the baseball game in the empty lot. Swing was replaced by jazz, which was replaced by rock, which was replaced by folk rock, which was replaced by acid rock, which was . . . The nickel Pepsi gave way to the fifty cent soda, and candy bars have gotten smaller while the price gets ever bigger. No matter the nostalgia, deep down we know we can't return. Going forward is a brave and courageous process.

Obviously, religion fits into all this, but not so neatly; it holds its own set of problems and questions. It is not at all what it used to be.

Just a short time ago, everybody seemed to have a religion, a faith by which they lived, more or less. It was something which we depended on. We appreciated the fact that it was there in hard times, and we celebrated good times through its structure. Religion seemed to give dignity to our lives, made us feel a part of something bigger. It gave reason for hope, and it helped us to bear the burdens of loss, sorrow, and failure. We had a kind of begrudging tolerance for those who didn't share our religious faith, yet we wouldn't condemn anyone for professing a different religion. But no matter the diverse differences between Protestants and Catholics, both found a peculiar harmony in condemning atheists and Godless people who professed no religion at all. We cautioned our children not to marry out of the church and certainly to avoid those who didn't believe in God.

Most of us didn't question the choice of religion which our parents had made for us. We accepted that and expected to live our lives the same way they did, hardly ever thinking about changing religion, converting, or ever giving it up altogether.

Conversions to other religions were exceptions, not rules. They usually took place because of marriage and spouses wanting to share the same faith. Sometimes a person was converted because of a strong association with someone who seemed to have a special insight, a sense of peaceful security because of what he or she believed. Sometimes persons of great stature were converted to another faith. Catholics were proud that G. K. Chesterton and John Henry Newman could be counted as converts to their ranks. But even so, conversion often raised eyebrows and caused a kind of sympathy for the naive character of the converted.

But suddenly, as though overnight, religion began to change drastically. Without people knowing exactly what was happening, faith and the practice of religion quietly lost their impact and diminished in the eyes of many people.

What was happening didn't admit of clear analysis. Simple answers to religious problems were wanting. It could be hoped at best that what was happening would be better understood at a later time. Some reasons were given, but they seemed only partial, unsatisfactory. Perhaps religion had lost its credibility from saying too much, overstating the words and doing less than what they said. Faithful people who had not questioned the church began to assert themselves, asking more from their ministers and leaders. They talked about gaps between what the church was and what Jesus had said it was supposed to be.

Another reason given for the declining state of religion was said to be technology and the remarkably swift progress in secular matters. Convenience appliances, television, higher living standards, the discoveries of science, and a general sense of victory over stubborn problems gave us all a sense of self-reliance and self-sufficiency. Trips to the moon and supersonic travel might have made God seem remote at best. People may have felt less guilty about judging that religion was not what it always said it was, a peaceful answer to all problems and the end of life's worries.

Technology brings a greater sense of freedom, takes at least some of the frustration from daily living, and manages to hide whatever loss is involved with apparent gains. If summer afternoon sociability has been replaced with scattering the family in various directions in various cars, the novelty seems good and it seems to compensate for what had to be sacrificed. If religious fervor has been overshadowed by the new age of progress, liberty is a welcome replacement for the old rigidity and the frustration of feeling that religion didn't clearly answer life's problems anyway.

Whatever the reasons might be, since the beginning of the 1960s we have witnessed a massive rethinking of religion and the place of God in American life. Without exaggeration, it is clear that overwhelming numbers of people have left the religion of their original choice and regrouped their spiritual forces in some way. To predict trends and point out directions is impossible. To explain this phenomenal transition in a paragraph or two would be supremely arrogant. What one knows is what one sees. There is no congregation which has not felt the impact of this reality. Where churches used to overflow with membership, seats are now easy to find, and the number of Sunday services has been reduced. If one objects that churches are still full, it is because they are in cities with high population and daily increases there. But per capita figures obviously reveal that church going is different for vast numbers of people. It has become sporadic, less habitual, and for many people, non-existent. There is no religion or sect which hasn't experienced this slump. Religion has changed, shifted from center, for many people.

One reaction to all this is a kind of panic and throwing up of hands by those who are working to maintain a state of balance and regain what has been lost. They are asking themselves where they went wrong and what can be done. Their general feeling is negative, a sense of failure. But some are beginning to see that criticism and rejection can be met with positive steps to improve what has gone before and to move in healthier directions. Some insights emerge right away. Religion must become more appealing, more attuned to the needs of today's world. Knowing why many have left religion should help us to respond to the needs of those who haven't and those who will some day return. It might be helpful to regard the confusion and exodus from religion as overdue and necessary to awaken in all of us a reevaluation of what religion can actually be expected to do in our lives. The God we propose to one another cannot be huffy, demanding obedience without reasons.

A general result of the recent religious upheaval has been a sincere search for ways to make religion more satisfying to the individual. This search, while at times frantic, has been taken up by many people, and a wide range of responses is offered to the same questions. Sometimes the answers are too simple, and the immediate solutions don't last. Because what is happening is so pervasive, a long time will be needed to sort it all out. But some trends are visible even now.

One of these trends is a strong recommendation to return to the basics. Some have said that if we would go backward rather than forward, our problems would be settled. We must think of how things were before, more serene and secure. Old time religion was better. When we get back to fundamentals, everything will be all right again. Radical thinking and liberalism must be avoided. Everything we need is contained in the Bible, God's word; it covers every situation. Examples of this kind of fundamentalism can be seen on Sunday morning television. Religious hours, with convincing preachers, sacred music, and a sense of the divine, are standard Sunday features. They are "well attended" and continue to grow in popularity. The startling difference between these programs and the religion of the past is that they demand even less participation. Religion is intellectual assent and belief in certain truths. Finding Jesus and being saved comes from conversion to "his ways." The world is divided between good and evil. What is important is identity with the "good" and rejection of what is "evil." The good resides in God's laws, the Bible, patriotism, love of country, and the upholding of tradition. Authority must always be respected. We must believe that God speaks especially to certain holy persons with the strong indication that those persons are ministers, those conducting the services. One is likely to hear phrases such as "Then the Lord said to me," or "God has asked me to tell you."

Fundamentalism is naive and simplistic. It leaves too much out and answers too few questions. It refuses to deal with certain problems: poverty, sickness, the abuses of political leaders, big business, and the oppressive plight of third world and persecuted countries. It at least implicitly holds that sickness and starvation arise through people's turning from God's will and that success and prosperity are the signal of God's blessing. Fundamentalism is characterized by well-dressed ministers in business suits. They touch people by the power of the spoken word at rallies and special gatherings. They have strong personal appeal and speak to the heart.

Many find something in this approach to religion. It gives them a sense of identity with countless people with whom they can share belief. Prayer and the Bible, long-standing hallmarks of religion, are sources of common expression. For these people, fundamentalism means an end of searching and confusion.

Related to fundamentalism but with its own shades of special meaning is the Jesus movement which has become so popular in our time. The rage to find Jesus shows the intensity of people's search for God and the gift of salvation. Proponents of this movement base their entire approach on the unconditional acceptance of Jesus as one's personal savior. The assurance that salvation comes through Jesus arises from the guarantee which Scripture offers. No one can be saved otherwise. It is the basic truth of religion. There is one way: "I am the way, the truth, and the life." Once we "find" this truth, all else becomes clear and completely simple. Life's problems are solved and we need only continue to accept this fundamental truth. The sureness of those who accept this belief can be perceived in the statements which they make: "I found it"; "I am a born again Christian"; "Since I found Jesus . . . ."

It is interesting to note that the Jesus movement has particular appeal to the young, those in high school, and somewhat beyond. While membership is not restricted to young people, they actually make up the majority of those who have accepted this way of life. This interest raises the question of how young people have become disillusioned with traditional religion. It indicates that what they have been taught, or perhaps not taught, has become unsatisfactory and pale. It further indicates that causes which really inspire people can ask almost anything of them.

If one wished to criticize the Jesus movement, he or she might begin by noting that it is very middle class. That would seem to be contrary to the intention of Jesus himself who said that he wanted to be identified with the poor and those in need of a physician. The so-called Jesus people seem less concerned about the needs of the poor and the sick who attracted Jesus so much. There seems to be a lack of social response in the movement to the problems of others. Acceptance and help seems to depend on one's incorporation into the movement. Motivation to join seems to be based on what the group does for the joiner without reference to what they can do for others. Conversion is required for reaping the benefits which God offers. Like other fundamentalists, Jesus people hold that once we accept Jesus our problems will be solved. If we wish proof of that, we need only look at the peace and prosperity of those who have endorsed the movement.

It cannot be denied that many people have found something positive in the Jesus movement. There is a strong sense of belonging among the members, a community spirit, a conviction of having arrived. Good feelings prevail at meetings and gatherings. Sometimes members experience kindness and sensitivity there after too little of those experiences in their work or family situations. Those who have been searching for security and a place to belong often find it here and are happy for the discovery. Sometimes more traditional religions have lacked these benefits.

Another manifestation of the continuing search for God can be seen in the charismatic movement. Those who have joined this movement have seen themselves as returning to the spirit of the early church. They emphasize St. Paul's teaching about the presence of the Spirit of God in the community. Each of us has special gifts which are given by God's providence and care for us. We might not allude to those gifts and live as though they were not there. If this is the case, we are not living truly spirit-filled lives as Jesus exhorted us to. In that case we simply give our religious faith and practice over to the church which then directs and leads us according to its laws and formulas. Without condemning the church, charismatics

contend that each of us has so much more within us that
only needs to be activated by asking the Spirit to bring
this beautiful lifestyle to reality.

They speak of baptism in the Spirit, asking for the
gifts and cultivating within oneself the faith necessary to
receive them. When this baptism takes effect, wonderful
things happen. At a gathering of charismatics, one is
likely to hear them speaking in tongues, prophesying,
interpreting what is said by others, and a general mur-
mur of praise and thanksgiving to God. One or other of
the members might pray for healing, and some might
maintain that they have actually been cured of illnesses.
The onlooker would see in the members a deep spirit of
concern for one another, for their needs, family situations,
and well-being. They would be willing to pray with anyone who wished and would offer genuine compassion. The
members would appear to be happy and to have overcome
much that is a concern to others. The sorrows and failures
which are so much a part of life are simply referred to
the Spirit of God in confidence and peace.

While being a charismatic calls for faith and enroll-
ment in the group, it does not become a religion in itself.
It is rather a feature of religion which can be integrated
into the lives of Protestants and Catholics alike. Charismatics, as well as other recent religious movements,
may well offer a better example of ecumenism than more
institutional religions do.

The criticism most often leveled at charismatics is
similar to that offered to other fundamental groups. Does
God, the Spirit, mean to solve our problems, live our lives
for us, or are we expected to grapple with the world ourselves? To give our lives over to the Spirit might take
away something which is properly ours as human beings.
If we are a community of people, responsible for one another, a united human family, then we should be concerned for the problems of all people as well as for our
own. If that is true, we must work at least as diligently
for those who are starving in third world countries, as

we do for those who are members of our charismatic group. Again, there seems to be a lack of broad social response on the part of charismatics to those outside.

Further criticism is offered in the fact that life is never as simple as some charismatics seem to believe. We cannot expect problems, sickness, poverty, addiction to drugs, and guilt over past sins to go away simply because we pray. Such an attitude does a disservice to God who created the resources in us to solve problems by direct confrontation with them. We have abilities and skills which we can call upon for our own good and the good of others. To rely on the Spirit so heavily might mean that we wouldn't use what is best in us. As a matter of fact, we do not solve problems but only cover them over when we refer them to someone outside ourselves. Psychology insists that each of us has to deal directly with what is problematic in us.

But there are many positive aspects to the charismatic movement. As it grows, people are becoming more conscious of the needs of those outside the group, the need to nurture others, to stand for what is needed, and to voice objection to what is abusive. As with other groups, there is a deep sense of community present in the members. Many persons whose lives have been unsatisfactory find a reason for being in the group; they feel a sense of acceptance and belonging which may have been lacking. For many, finding the group means greater happiness than ever before in their lives.

One aspect of the modern upheaval in religion is the proliferation of a variety of sects. Sects are generally based on the notion that there is a certain secret or key to living which once acquired opens up a whole new dimension of awareness. Sects differ from religions in that they demand obedience to living persons. The leaders of sects are believed to be mediums through whom one acquires the secrets of life. They possess obscure knowledge which cannot be gained in ordinary ways. Members of sects are taught to trust their leaders to such a degree that their lives belong to another. Members of sects happily spend their energies furthering the cause which is voiced through the leaders, working daily, proselytizing, selling goods, and begging assistance. They reject whatever is contrary to the objectives of the sect.

Many people today, especially young people, are strongly attracted to sects. They offer refuge from the ordinary cares of life, giving attractive alternatives to much which can be disturbing in the world. The healthy existence of so many sects seems to testify that there are deep and unfulfilled longings in many people today. Sects propose to offer comfort for the loneliness and desperation in life. Those with deep problems are naturally attracted to whatever offers the hope of peace and security.

But the price is high. It almost always means rejection of family and friends, abandoning normal lifestyles, and giving complete allegiance to the leader and the other members of the group. Indoctrination is so profound that members are often thought to lose something of their own will and become brainwashed. It is sometimes impossible to establish reasonable communication with members of sects. They seem to have certain blind spots which cannot be penetrated. Those who accept membership often cause much sorrow in the lives of their former associates.

There are other groups which are made up of people who support a given cause, and that gives them a unity. Such groups are almost beyond number and many have something of a religious fervor to them. This arises from a deep conviction that the cause is worthy of support and dedication. Such a group might espouse greater care for the environment, the banning of nuclear weapons, more help for the poor, more sensitive treatment of prisoners, and so on.

Within these groups there is often the same conviction and dedication that is found in religious belief. There might also be a blatant irreverence for the customs and values of society in these people. But one cannot deny that they are in touch with basic issues which are sometimes neglected by groups which profess to be religious. Organized religion too often ignores the abuses which demand recognition in our society. If members of these groups are not consciously searching for God, they are certainly involved in a quest for that which is lasting and rises above what is common and passing.

The search for God and for meaning goes on, and undoubtedly it exists in everyone. Some seek God in a more organized fashion. They remain in contact with the religion of their parents and find satisfaction in their local church. Others ask for change within the church and welcome what has made their lives more meaningful through the renewal of doctrine and practice. Some people have become more acutely aware that every religion should demand more from its members in response to the needs of others.

The growing phenomenon of religious quest and the almost daily multiplication of groups which offer the assurance of peace to their members indicate a great deal. There is a tremendous hunger in each of us for acceptance, regard, and recognition. In our sometimes frantic pursuit of technological answers and convenient living, we have neglected the deeper social needs which all people experience. We might have expected technology and science to take care of these needs. But we are awakening to the fact that we have missed some important considerations.

There is much we are learning. Religion has its own contribution to offer. The gospel message exhorts the follower of Jesus to continue to give to the world what he himself gave. As we begin to respond to that message, religion becomes credible to many more people and even to those who had judged that Christianity had little to offer to them. Jesus came saying we must love, not conditionally, but without reservation. He said that we could possess the whole world and still miss the point of living. There is ample evidence that for many people this is the case. We might have beautiful homes, be wealthy, enjoy power over others, be given honors for our accomplishments, and still be personally unhappy.

The discovery of God can come to us in obscure places where we might never have expected it to happen. We might see God's features more clearly in the faces of the poor, those with insurmountable problems, those who look to us for assistance. We might find our search ending in the discovery that religion offers us a way to celebrate what has already happened in our lives. We go to church, join a group, and practice our religion, not because we are seeking something, but because we have found it deep within ourselves, in others, in care for and response to all persons. We come to say we are glad we have found God and we want to offer that good news to those who are also seeking.

Religion isn't what it used to be. It should be more. It must be growing, renewing itself, revealing God in everyday life, in what we do alone, and in what we are doing for others.

When several of the apostles were following Jesus after his baptism, he suddenly turned to them and asked, "What do you want?" They asked in turn, "Where are we going?" Jesus then responded, "Come and see." It is going and seeing which comprise the search. Religion never implies standing still, waiting for something to happen. It must be going to see and making things happen because Jesus said it was possible. It is possible to renew the face of the earth. But only if we go and see.